Our efforts to express blessing to others often become routine and trite. However, reading this book will awaken the spirit to the power of words of blessing.

GARY D. CHAPMAN, author of *The 5 Love Languages*

I started reading Tina Boesch's book like a freight train rushing to its destination. Instead, I found myself on a slow hike, immersing myself in the words that caused me to observe Scripture and principles of blessing in a new way. Her words left me captivated with a desire to be like Jacob and wrestle with God until receiving a blessing.

KELLY KING, manager of magazines/devotional publishing and women's ministry training at LifeWay Christian Resources

Tina tells the biblical story with great attention to narrative detail and has chosen her examples astutely. Interwoven with all this are many wonderful stories from her own and others' lives, which illuminate the themes she's trying to get across.

IAIN W. PROVAN, Marshall Sheppard Professor of Biblical Studies at Regent College

In our day, "blessing" has sadly been reduced to a hashtag, frequently used in a shallow or braggadocio way. But in *Given*, Tina Boesch unpacks the richness of the biblical meaning of blessing. Her writing is exquisite, poetic, and rooted in the biblical narrative. In the truest sense of the word, Tina has richly blessed the family of God with her book. I highly recommend!

SUSIE HAWKINS, speaker and author of *From One Ministry Wife to Another: Honest Conversations about Ministry Connections*

Tina Boesch can bless in a wide range of modes: artist, art scholar, tour guide, theological teacher, evangelist, hostess, daughter, sister, friend, wife, mother, and more. This beautiful book comes from a heart ready to bless, a mind brimming with good things, and a mouth able to put things fitly, "like apples of gold in a setting of silver" (Proverbs 25:11)—all bundled with a strong back, capable hands, and a quick smile. Come and be blessed!

> **JOHN G. STACKHOUSE, JR.**, Samuel J. Mikolaski Professor of Religious Studies at Crandall University

Given is a book that should not be ignored. In it, Tina Boesch explores the biblically significant notion of "blessing." Rejecting both the prosperity gospel's reduction of "blessing" to economic success and many evangelicals' reduction of it to some sort of vague future hope, she argues that the ultimate expression of blessing is the Cross, where Christ gave himself on our behalf, blessing us so that we could bless others—even our enemies. In a delightful and surprising manner, *Given* not only explores the richness of biblical teaching but also takes the reader on a journey through history and across the globe. Highly recommended.

> **BRUCE ASHFORD**, dean of faculty at Southeastern Baptist Theological Seminary and author of *Letters to an American Christian*

A year or so ago, I was led to Tina Boesch's blog and soon found myself binge-reading her posts. She has a tremendous way with the English language—her prose is redolent, Christ centered, even pungent at times, but always winsome. And this book is no exception. I have long thought that blessings and benedictions are a lost art among evangelicals, and Tina's book is the very thing we need to recover a vital part of our heritage. May it be widely read, appreciated, and put into practice!

MICHAEL A. G. HAYKIN, professor of church history at Southern Baptist Theological Seminary

Given brings back the soul songs we should've been singing to each other for centuries. It's like a deep breath that pulls the reader into a place of rest, a place where God himself and his goodness is enough—a place where we live to share that goodness with others.

GRACE THORNTON, author of *I Don't Wait Anymore: Letting Go of Expectations and Grasping God's Adventure for You*

What the next generation looks for is legacy. How do the decisions we make today affect their tomorrows? In this book, Tina talks about what's obvious and not-so-obvious in the legacy of blessing that we offer to those in our lives. Her perspective is practical and demonstrated through history and personal experience. If we're able to extend that hope to others, we hold a gift few fully comprehend.

REGGIE JOINER, founder and CEO at Orange

Dear Denise, (Gold Digger)
Don't ever forget that you're
a Blessing to Jesus and Me and
Others! God Bless You My!
Love,
Ruby V.
7-3-19

given

THE FORGOTTEN MEANING
AND PRACTICE OF BLESSING

• • •

TINA BOESCH

A NavPress resource published in alliance
with Tyndale House Publishers, Inc.

NavPress is the publishing ministry of The Navigators, an international Christian organization and leader in personal spiritual development. NavPress is committed to helping people grow spiritually and enjoy lives of meaning and hope through personal and group resources that are biblically rooted, culturally relevant, and highly practical.

For more information, visit www.NavPress.com.

Given: The Forgotten Meaning and Practice of Blessing

Copyright © 2019 by Kristina Boesch. All rights reserved.

A NavPress resource published in alliance with Tyndale House Publishers, Inc.

NAVPRESS is a registered trademark of NavPress, The Navigators, Colorado Springs, CO. The NAVPRESS logo is a trademark of NavPress, The Navigators. *TYNDALE* is a registered trademark of Tyndale House Publishers, Inc. Absence of ® in connection with marks of NavPress or other parties does not indicate an absence of registration of those marks.

The Team:
Don Pape, Publisher
David Zimmerman, Acquisitions Editor
Elizabeth Schroll, Copy Editor
Dean H. Renninger, Designer

Cover painting by Dean H. Renninger; copyright © Tyndale House Publishers, Inc.; all rights reserved. Author photo by Josh Bourgeois; used by permission.

Published in association with the literary agency of Wolgemuth & Associates, Inc.

Some of the anecdotal illustrations in this book are true to life and are included with the permission of the persons involved. All other illustrations are composites of real situations, and any resemblance to people living or dead is purely coincidental.

For information about special discounts for bulk purchases, please contact Tyndale House Publishers at csresponse@tyndale.com, or call 1-800-323-9400.

Cataloging-in-Publication Data is available.

ISBN 978-1-63146-973-2

Printed in the United States of America

25	24	23	22	21	20	19
7	6	5	4	3	2	1

For Brett, who chose to make home with me,

and

for my parents, Paula and Ken Hemphill,

who first introduced me to the shine.

"May your hearts live forever!"

PSALM 22:26

contents

chapter 1

BLESSING IN THE BEGINNING

INTO RELATIONSHIP

Life be in my speech,
Sense in what I say,
The bloom of cherries on my lips,
Till I come back again.
The love Christ Jesus gave
Be filling every heart for me,
The love Christ Jesus gave
Filling me for every one.

TRADITIONAL SCOTTISH BLESSING,
NINETEENTH CENTURY

There are conversations that hang in the air. Some words dissipate like vapor, but others linger, their full force felt weeks, months, or even years later, as they settle in our minds and hearts. Having taken up residence, they push us into unexplored territories. Some conversations acquire a life all their own. One such conversation launched my search to understand the meaning of blessing.

I remember the clear winter day and the aching of the ash-colored branches stoic in the cold outside my apartment. I remember the cast of light slanting through the windows and the crisp outlines of buildings framing the glittering waters of the Bosporus, the strait that divides Europe and Asia and runs through the heart of Istanbul, Turkey. And I remember the earnest look of delight on my friend's bright face as we talked about my sister and her new baby.

We sat on my couch, relaxed in faded jeans and sock feet. As we chatted in Turkish, I sensed my friend's earnest joy—she longed to see the baby, to speak with my sister, to wish her well, to bless her. I soon found myself pushing aside delicate, tulip-shaped chai glasses to make space for my laptop on the coffee table in front of us so that we could video chat on Skype.

Just before we called, my friend paused. She wasn't confident she would say the right thing. So she asked me what to say in English to someone who's just had a baby. I replied matter-of-factly, "We say, 'Congratulations.'"

My Muslim friend looked dubious. "No," she pressed, "I mean what do Christians say *as a blessing*?"

I paused, bewildered by the pointedness of her question. I repeated, "Honestly, we just say, 'Congratulations.'"

Her brow knit, betraying her frustration. I could see disappointment hovering in her eyes. "You say congratulations all the time," she observed. "'Congratulations' *isn't* a blessing."

She was right. "Congratulations" *isn't* a blessing.

In Turkish, the gracious thing to say on the occasion of the birth of a baby is *Analı babalı büyütsün*. Roughly translated, the words mean, "May you grow up together with your mother and father." The blessing conveyed by that concise phrase is magnificent. So much good is expressed by a simple, compact blessing. The phrase efficiently encapsulates a prayer for the health and protection of the baby, for the long life of the mother and father, and for the integrity of the family. No wonder "Congratulations" was a disappointment.

I certainly don't mean to say that "Congratulations" is a bad sentiment; it's just a thin one. *Congratulations*, a word with Latin roots and a Middle English pedigree, means that I share your joy, I give thanks with you.[1] Celebrating with friends and rejoicing with those who rejoice is vital; it's a basic minimum for any relationship. But "Congratulations" is of the moment—it references only how I'm feeling now; it doesn't reach forward into what will be, into the good I hope to see unfold in the future. And it doesn't invite God to be present in our lives by expressing what he may accomplish in the days to come.

The future is the province of blessing. Blessings are prayers with the horizon in view. They communicate good that I long to see realized in your life, and they acknowledge, implicitly, that God alone is capable of accomplishing that good. Blessings carry us from the present moment into future grace.

"Blessing . . ." reflects the poet John O'Donohue, "animates on the deepest threshold between being and becoming."[2]

While the conversation with my Turkish friend was simmering in my mind, I was learning to do life with my family in one of the most storied cities in the world—Istanbul, Turkey. I've lived most of the last twenty years overseas—in Italy, Bulgaria, Cyprus, and most recently, Turkey. Crossing cultures shakes me out of familiar, comfortable patterns of speaking and thinking, challenging me to acquire new ways of expressing myself that sometimes cast a clarifying light on the world.

As I was blundering my way through learning Turkish, I began to realize that many basic phrases I was using every day were simple blessings. To a baker making a traditional pastry: *Elinize sağlık*, "Health to your hands." To a neighbor coming down with a cold: *Geçmiş olsun*, "May it pass." To a bride at her wedding: *Bir yastıkta kocayın*, "May you sleep together on the same pillow." To a student beginning the school year: *Hayırlı olsun*, "May it be successful." To a friend leaving on a long drive: *Yolun açık olsun*, "May the way be open" (a blessing needed in a city of about fifteen million where gridlock is part of daily life). Sometimes, I heard the greeting that is also a profound blessing, *Selamun aleyküm*, "Peace be with you."

Peace be with you—those words have such a powerful resonance. After Jesus' resurrection, they were the first words Jesus spoke to his disciples, who were cowering together in a locked room, immobilized by fear. He greeted them with a blessing of peace and then he commissioned them with the same blessing, saying, "*Peace be with you!* As the Father has sent me, I am sending you" (John 20:21, NIV, emphasis added). This peace is much more than a wish for the absence of conflict; this peace annihilates fear, heals brokenness, and restores relationship. This is the peace of *shalom*, a well-being that embraces body, mind, and soul, one that knits individuals together into flourishing community.

Or at least, that's what it should be. But the reality is that the words we say too often tend to lose their potency. When a blessing is reduced to a phrase we say out of habit, then it's drained of its significance. A blessing should be a sincere prayer that rises from our souls. When giving a blessing evolves into saying what we're expected to in a given situation, then it might be better not to say it at all. Perhaps this is the reason why some churches have abandoned the Christian practice of the sharing of peace during worship. I suspect they did so out of recognition that the people in the pews, arena seats, or folding chairs turning to greet their neighbors were mouthing words that no longer conveyed the good they were meant to embody. When the blessing of peace becomes a conventional greeting synonymous with "hello" in Christian fellowship, we should consider whether we've forgotten the depth of meaning the blessing originally encapsulated.

Before I moved to a culture in which blessing is woven into everyday social interactions, I paid no attention whatsoever to the role blessing played in the Bible and in God's history with his people. Western culture is so thoroughly secularized that it has, for the most part, long been stripped of the language of blessing. In public conversations, the remnants of blessing have been reduced to meaningless cliché, a reality that is best illustrated by the reflexive instinct to say

"Bless you" after a sneeze. Even in religious circles, blessing doesn't pack much of a punch. I grew up hearing polite, silver-haired ladies exclaim, "Honey, bless your heart"—a sentimental expression that often conveys genuine affection and sometimes a hint of gentle dismissal, but never a sense of power and purpose.

There are a lot of mixed messages out there about blessing. On one hand, some people seem to think blessing is material—health, wealth, status, palatial homes, private jets, and the freedom to relax, settle into a lounge chair, and savor the benefits of the "good" life. This is the message underlying the prosperity gospel, religion that encourages people to cash in with God. Manipulative preachers line their pockets while convincing people to give generously in order to "receive a blessing" in return. On the other hand, some spiritualize blessing to the point that it doesn't have any real implication for living in the world. Blessing becomes a vague future hope—a heavenly reward, but not a present reality. Which is the true meaning of God's blessing? Material or spiritual? Is God's blessing for now or for later?

I suspect that these approaches to understanding the meaning and practice of blessing don't exactly jive with the picture painted in Scripture. Navigating the confusion around blessing will require going back to the source, a deep dive into God's Word. Scripture is by nature as confrontational as it is comforting. And it is confronting me with the challenge of getting to the bottom of the meaning of a concept I had basically written off.

I'll have to work to unearth the relationship between blessing and God's mission if I want to understand its relevance for my life. I long to understand all that the call to bless means, not just theoretically but also practically. How do the complex characters we meet in Scripture bless one another? Does the Bible offer any blessings that can be woven into daily life? Do I know how to bless my husband, my kids, my friends, my neighbors? Am I prepared to embrace the sharp edge of blessing—Jesus' call to bless those who curse? How to become a river, not a reservoir, of God's blessing?

There's so much distrust in our world these days, but blessings have a way of breaking through the unease because they give voice to the intentions of a heart that desires abundant life for others. Abundant life is such a fundamental blessing that when I open the Bible in search of blessing, it's the first one I find.

The Origin of Blessing

The first blessing in the Bible shows up in the first chapter of the first book—Genesis. The Hebrew root of the word "bless"—*barak*—is used eighty-eight times in Genesis, more than in any other Old Testament book.[3] Only the frequency of usage in the Psalms and Deuteronomy even comes close. The preeminence of blessing as an essential theme in the book that sets the stage for all that follows is reinforced by its appearance right at the start of the Creation story.

Appreciating the power of blessing begins with recognizing the generative power of the spoken word. In Genesis, there's no more vital power than God's word. God speaks and sparks fly, electrifying the empty darkness. God's word calls being into existence and transforms chaotic nothingness into organic, ordered beauty. Over the course of seven days, God's word is a creative force. Every time God speaks, a new reality is born.

While not quite conforming to the norms of Hebrew poetry, there's a lyrical, hymnic quality to the first chapter of Genesis that makes me feel as though I'm listening to music scored on a cosmic scale:

> *God said*
> *and it was so,*
> *God saw*
> *that it was good,*
> *and there was evening*
> *and there was morning,*
> *a new day dawns.*

With the dawn, I pause, breathe in, and prepare for the next movement. This pattern is repeated through the first four days, but then there's one critical addition to the refrain. On the final three days of Creation, God blesses. It's not until God makes living, breathing beings that he speaks blessing. Observing the oceans and sky roiling with new life, Genesis 1:22 says, "And *God blessed them*, saying, 'Be fruitful and multiply and fill the waters in the seas, and let birds multiply on the earth'" (emphasis added).

The first blessing in the Bible is life that flourishes and makes more life: *Be fruitful and multiply.* My entire life I've read these words as a command, but now I realize they are a blessing. God isn't barking out an order to obey, he's bestowing a gift of abundant life to receive. How I read this first interaction between God and his creation is bound to shape my impression of the character of the Creator revealed in these verses.

In Genesis, God creates *and* he blesses—two distinct but marvelously complementary actions. His creative word is the source of life in the present, and his blessing of fruitfulness and multiplication—of fertility and abundance—is the wellspring of our future existence. God's blessing propels life forward—it is the "vital, effective power that makes the future possible."[4] God's blessing is more than a wish, more than a hope—it's a positive statement of what will be. God is not saying that life *should* multiply; he's saying that life *will* multiply.

Folded within God's blessing is a promise of what will become reality: It prophetically reaches into the future. If we read the early chapters of Genesis in light of the entire book, we find that God's blessing is unfailingly effective. Genealogies give structure to the narrative and testify to the vitality of his blessing of fertility. Adam, Noah, Esau, and Jacob all saw their family lines multiply. Jacob alone could count sixty-six direct descendants (Genesis 46:26). Blessing dovetails with prophecy in the way both lean into the future. Blessing breathes newness into our spirits by enabling us to envision a path forward with God, a new reality toward which we will move in faith. As Walter Brueggemann puts it, "We are energized not by that which we already possess but by that which is promised and about to be given."[5] God's blessing energizes us because it touches on what will be given, lifting us from present reality into future grace.

God's blessing is an essential, vital power for life, and when God's blessing is directed *to* us, it's also an invitation to relationship. When God creates man and woman in his own image, he not only speaks a blessing *over* them but also speaks blessing *to* them. In Genesis 1:28, when God first addresses Adam and Eve, the addition of a preposition that wasn't there in God's blessing of the animals is significant: "God said *to* them, 'Be fruitful and multiply'" (emphasis added).

On the fifth day, when God blesses the birds and the fish, he doesn't speak blessing *to* them the way he does to Adam and Eve. God's relationship with human beings would be different from his relationship to other living creatures. He speaks a blessing *to* man and woman; he converses *with* them. He gifts them with the responsibility of cultivating the Garden and caring for the animals inhabiting it, and later he walks alongside them in the cool of the day. This personal interaction distinguishes God's relationship with man and woman, who bear his image.

God's blessing is intimately relational because it invites communion. "The God who speaks through the Word," says Jacques Ellul, "is neither far off nor abstract. Rather, he is the creator by means of something that is primarily a means of relationship. . . . The God who creates through the Word is not outside his creation, but with it, and especially with Adam, who is made precisely in order to hear this very word and create this relationship with God. Having received the Word himself, Adam can respond to God *in dialogue*."[6]

God's blessing of man and woman is the first movement in a conversation. It's the opening of a dialogue with humanity. Genesis shows us that when God reaches out to us with blessing, he speaks first. If we're listening, we're free to respond either with blessing and obedience or with indifference and disobedience. We hear the reverberations of the right response sung in Psalm 103: "Bless the LORD, O my soul, and all that is within me, bless his holy name!" The appropriate, faithful response to God's blessing is doxology—worship.

Before God's blessing is material or spiritual, it's relational. Before anything else, God's blessing invites us into relationship with him, which is also the genesis of abundant life with others. The primal blessing of fruitfulness and multiplication is observable, physical, social. It's earthy, even sensual, in the way it requires the involvement of our bodies. There's no multiplication of life without touch, without intimacy, without sex. By blessing physical intimacy between husband and wife with fruitfulness, God affirms the essential goodness of living an embodied, relational existence.

Blessing Interrupted: The Birth of Curse

I remember sitting uncomfortably on a rust-colored vinyl couch waiting for a doctor to confirm my first pregnancy. I didn't look pregnant, but I felt awful. Morning sickness never seemed to be confined to the morning. When I met the doctor who would shepherd me through the nine-month journey, he handed me his card, which proudly displayed the promise "Painless childbirth." I wondered if it could be true.

Now I know that it was a hollow slogan, so hilariously out of touch with reality that only a detached observer of the process who was overly confident in the numbing effects of modern medicine could have written it. Since then, I've had three babies and three entirely different birthing experiences, but I wouldn't describe any of them as painless. If God first blessed physical multiplication, what's gone so wrong?

Although Adam and Eve first lived in Eden in a state of blessedness suffused with God's presence, it wasn't long before another voice started speaking in the Garden. An insidious serpentine voice twisted the word of God in a way that caused Eve to question the goodness of her Maker. As Creator, God has the authority to set parameters for living in his blessing. Adam and Eve didn't live in a world of their own making—they inhabited one given to them as a trust.

In Eden, God laid down the most minimal of boundaries. He gave the fruit of every tree in the Garden for food, save one—the tree of the knowledge of good and evil. The serpent tempted Eve to taste the fruit from this tree. Temptation inspired doubt: "Did God actually say . . . ?" Doubt gave way to desire. Desire inspired transgression. And so, in the middle of a garden filled with delicious fruit growing on countless trees, Eve fixated on the fruit from the one and only tree that hadn't been given. Then she grasped the object of her desire and gave it to her husband. Together, Adam and Eve were saying through their taking that God's blessing of abundant provision wasn't enough. They wanted more. So rather than graciously receive all the good that had been given, they seized what had been forbidden. In that moment, they stepped out of God's blessing and into curse.

First off, it's important to note that God is not the source of the curse in the way he's the origin of blessing. God initiates blessing. He spoke blessing before Adam and Eve asked for it, before they even knew they needed it. But the curse entered creation as a consequence of human action defying

God's direction. Curse is the result of rebellion. God granted Adam and Eve agency to follow him or to go their own way, to obey or disobey. They chose the latter. So the curse is the result of sin—it's God's judgment of human defiance.

To Eve, God said,

> I will make your pains in childbearing very severe;
> with painful labor you will give birth to children.
> Your desire will be for your husband,
> and he will rule over you.
>
> GENESIS 3:16, NIV

In Eve's case, the curse tinges her most intimate experiences—childbearing and her interaction with her husband. The miraculous process of conceiving, birthing, and raising children—the central focus of God's initial blessing—now becomes laced with severe pain. The relationship between husband and wife, the two who should have been unified as one, is now tainted with power politics and shame. Because of the curse, there are fissures where there should have been wholeness, dominance and submission where there should have been union. In the words of Bruce Waltke, "Control has replaced freedom; coercion has replaced persuasion; division has replaced multiplication."[7]

To Adam, God said,

> Cursed is the ground because of you;
> through painful toil you will eat food from it
> all the days of your life.
> It will produce thorns and thistles for you,

> and you will eat the plants of the field.
> By the sweat of your brow
> you will eat your food
> until you return to the ground.
>
> GENESIS 3:17-19, NIV

God's blessing produces abundance, but curse causes scarcity. Now thistles and thorns crop up in place of nourishing harvest. The delightful mission of caring for the earth and cultivating the Garden is transformed into painful toil.

Taken together, the effects of the curse are tension between men and women, discord where there had been harmony, alienation from God, and exile from the Garden. The bottom line: The curse devastates the environment and, most crucially, the most meaningful relationships.

But even within the judgment of the curse, there's mercy. God speaks directly to the serpent, saying, "Cursed are you" (Genesis 3:14). But his address to Adam is oblique: "*Cursed is the ground* because of you." God doesn't allow the consequences of Adam and Eve's sin to cancel his primal blessing. Men and women will still be fruitful and multiply, but now the experience that would have been only blessing will be infused with pain. Humans will still tend the earth, but the work that would have been done in a lush garden will be done in an unyielding environment. God's blessing endures, but rebelling against God's goodness has consequences. And it's not just Adam and Eve who felt them; we feel them too.

Feeling the Curse

Here I am living thousands of years after the curse was first pronounced, the beneficiary of centuries of technological and scientific breakthroughs from ultrasounds to anesthesia, and I still suffer its effects. The nausea, the contractions, the labor, the sutures, the abbreviated nights, the sore everything, the patience stretched thin by crying and colic and later by tantrums, the confusion about how to parent well, the distance I've felt from my husband and from my former self, the stress of providing for our children in an unyielding economic environment—here's the total package of pain embodied in the curse.

One of my kids—my two-year-old, *my baby*—hasn't slept well in two years. Night after night, I find myself padding across the hall to comfort her and end up wedged into her tiny toddler bed. The punishing physical exhaustion takes a toll on my marriage. I feel splintered, my patience whittled down, my judgment blurred. I sense myself withdrawing from the man I married. Our responses to each other are clipped. Our words bristle. The chill between us is only intensified by his quiet nature—he's not a man to vent his feelings. He detaches through silence, not by control or meanness. Here we are feeling the curse.

Leaning on the kitchen counter by the sink, I can feel the cold of the white marble floor through my slippers. My husband sits in a chair pulled up to our tiny wooden kitchen table. His forehead rests on his hand; his shoulders sag. It's been a hard day. Both of us are spent in our own ways—depleted, poured out. But as we talk, the severe edges of our conversation soften. I move over to him and lay my hands on his shoulders and I pray blessing. I speak the good I long for him out loud. The distance closes a little. And I can feel a reorientation, a turning in my mind and heart. Instead of staying mired in my frustration, I look toward where I hope we're headed. We lean in. We move toward each other and move together toward God. Blessing—the antidote to curse.

I can't even begin to conceive of the regret Adam and Eve must have felt as they stumbled out of the Garden. They might have left empty-handed, but their hearts were loaded with a terrible burden. They knew that the curse would affect not only their own lives but also the lives of their children and their children's children. The pain of childbirth and the hardening of the ground was nothing compared to the pain of fractured relationships and the loss of intimacy with God.

In *Paradise Lost*, an epic portrayal of the first few chapters of Genesis, John Milton gives voice to Adam's despair.

> *Accurst of blessed? Hide me from the face*
> *Of God.*
> *All that I eat or drink, or shall beget,*
> *Is propagated curse.*

As Adam ponders the terrible inheritance of brokenness that he's leaving behind, an impossible thought occurs to him: He wishes that he could take the curse upon himself so the world could live in God's blessing.

> *. . . in me all*
> *Posterity stands cursed: fair patrimony*

That I must leave ye, Sons! O, were I able
To waste it all myself, and leave ye none!
So disinherited, how would you bless
Me, now your curse![8]

Milton's imaginative portrayal of Adam's longing to spare future generations from the curse foreshadows the reality that one day, a new Man—*a new Adam*—will take upon himself the curse introduced by the first. His sacrificial act will free men and women from the power of the curse and the grip of sin and death.

How to return again to the original state, when relationships were whole and healthy and all was blessing? In many ways, this longing animates the story of the Bible—*return*. In God's judgment, he said that Adam would "return to the ground," but Adam must have yearned to return to God's blessing. How to return to the goodness of living in God's presence? How to be free of the curse? How to return to a state of relationship where man and woman live with one another, naked and unashamed, souls exposed but completely safe? How to live without anxiety, fear, division, dominance, sin, and the shadow of death? The hope of abolishing curse signifies the resolution to these questions because blessing won't return until the power of curse is canceled.

Given to Bless

The hills around Assisi, Italy, are dressed with the shimmering sage gray of olive leaves and the deep green of citrus groves. There aren't many tall trees, save for the elegant

Italian cypress. The wilderness doesn't feel very wild. Even though it's been years since I walked the paths meandering through those hills, I still recall the surprise of stumbling on a tiny, handmade cross, two twigs bound together by a stalk of grass. Holding the delicate symbol, I noticed another leaning beside the base of a tree trunk, then another balanced precariously on a tree limb. Because they were all made of bits of branch, they blended seamlessly into their environment. But once I knew what to look for, I began finding them everywhere—tiny testaments to God's glory tucked into unexpected places all across the landscape.

These diminutive crosses were left by pilgrims who came to visit the place where God called Francis of Assisi into a life of poverty and prayer. Before Francis was a monk, he was the son of a nobleman. Rich, privileged, and irresponsible, Francis was an unlikely ascetic. But an irresistible call and an undeniable vision of Christ transformed him. He renounced his wealth, physically stripping down to nothing in front of his father and a crowd of concerned townspeople.

A depiction of this public moment of decision appears frescoed on the wall of the Basilica of Saint Francis in the heart of Assisi. The fresco is one in a cycle of paintings made in the mid-thirteenth century usually attributed to Giotto di Bondone, whose naturalistic style became an inspiration to Renaissance masters like Michelangelo. In Giotto's painting, Francis stands with empty hands raised heavenward. A disembodied hand floats in the heavens, representing the presence of God. The index and middle fingers of God's hand are extended in a gesture that medieval Italians would have immediately recognized as a sign of blessing.[9]

The painting is a statement that by renouncing material wealth, Francis was determined to live solely dependent on God's blessing. And that is precisely what Francis did. He lived the rest of his life dedicated to God, excruciatingly poor and blazingly happy. His life reveals that having nothing at all isn't at odds with being blessed most of all because being blessed means living sustained by God's presence.

The crosses I found hidden in the woods surrounding Francis's hillside retreat testify to the monk's deep desire to identify with Christ by being crucified with him. Their location—outside in nature rather than confined to a church's interior—reflect his renowned friendly familiarity with the created world. In his solitude, Francis was said to preach to the birds, encouraging them to praise the one who made them. Francis didn't so much preach as sing. In G. K. Chesterton's estimation, "He was a poet whose whole life was a poem."[10] He lived longing to walk with God in a world that was both garden and temple.

One episode in Francis's life that isn't well known is his venture into the camp of the sultan of Egypt, Malik al-Kamil. In a letter written in 1220 to the abbess of the Cistercian convent of Aywières, a priest named Jacques de Vitry described Francis of Assisi's 1219 visit to the crusader camp in Damietta on the Nile delta in Egypt. Jacques expressed concern about the dangers of Francis's plan to meet with the sultan, since he was unlikely to return from this mission alive. Francis, however, was undeterred because he believed that God's blessing was intended not just for Europeans but for the whole world.[11]

I'm reading about Francis's brave (some would say foolhardy) ventures while staying at a retreat center in the foothills of the Blue Ridge Mountains. It's winter and the trees are bare. I wake up in the silence before dawn. In the velvet black of very early morning, I'm sitting in an octagonal room with windows on nearly every side. Part of the reason I'm here is that I've been wrestling with the rootless nature of the life I believe was given to me. To begin to understand the inheritance of blessing that accompanies a demanding call away from home, I'll soon turn to study Abraham, a man destined to be a river of blessing that would flow to cover all the families of the earth. But right now, the glow of a lamp illuminates a page from Thomas Merton's *The New Man*:

> To find the full meaning of our existence we must find not the meaning that we expect but the meaning that is revealed to us by God. . . .
>
> Meaning is then not something we discover in ourselves, or in our lives. The meanings we are capable of discovering are never sufficient. The true meaning has to be revealed. It has to be "given" . . . *for life itself is, in the end, only significant in so far as it is given.*[12]

Glancing up from the book, over my right shoulder, I can see a pink glow beginning to warm the trunks of the oaks. I turn my head, looking now to the east, and I can see the first spark of amber warming the horizon through the tangle of bald branches. This dawn is *given*. This beauty is given as a gift, offered as blessing. I take a cue from this overture, realizing that I'm being invited to respond to the one who gives.

Bless the Lord, O my soul,
and everything within me
bless your holy name.

May every thought,
every word,
every impulse,
the whole of my inner being,
my way of relating to you throughout the day
bless your holy name.

Mend the cursed fractures caused by resistance to your will,
forgive my grasping, my taking.
May the world as it is
be transformed into the world that was meant to be
one word, one confession, one grace at a time,
until we return
to you.

chapter 2

BLESSING THAT FREES US TO FOLLOW

LETTING GO

The keeping of God upon thee in every pass,
The shielding of Christ upon thee in every path,
The bathing of the Spirit upon thee in every stream,
In every land and sea thou goest.

A CELTIC BLESSING

When the tram lights illuminated only an empty field, I knew I was in trouble. As soon as the driver switched off the lights and started climbing down the steps, I panicked.

I jumped up from my seat near the back of the tram and dashed forward, mumbling an incomprehensible greeting in a language I was only beginning to learn. The semester of Czech I had taken fall of my sophomore year in college hadn't prepared me for this moment.

It was nearly midnight, and I was somewhere on the outskirts of Bratislava, Slovakia. Earlier in the evening, I had met two friends for dinner in the city center. They directed me to the last tram headed to the outskirts of town for the night, unjustifiably confident that it would take me straight to my stop. But I had only arrived in the city a week earlier and was still getting a feel for the lay of the land. Up until then, I had only ridden the tram in daylight, when the contours of the buildings were more recognizable. In the dark, all the Soviet-era block apartments looked exactly the same. My stop had come and gone.

I'd never felt so utterly alone. I was a nineteen-year-old foreigner with no clue how to return to the apartment where I was staying that summer. I was totally vulnerable and completely desperate.

The driver nearly jumped out of his skin when he saw me. He hadn't even known I was there. As I sputtered broken phrases, feebly attempting to explain my predicament, his expression softened. And then he laughed. Not a derisive laugh. Not a predatory laugh. He laughed like a grandfather amused by the antics of a toddler. Still shaking his head in weary amusement, he sat back down in the driver's seat and switched on the lights. The tram shuddered and moved forward. He patiently backtracked through the route until I recognized my stop.

When I was home safe, I locked the apartment door behind me. Then I dropped to my knees with gratitude— thankful for the kindness of the driver, thankful for the kindness of God. Some might say I had been lucky. But I tend to believe I was blessed.

Cross-cultural travel always makes me feel vulnerable. As a foreigner in a strange land, I am dislocated, exposed, confused in a way I never would be if I stayed safely within the borders of my home country. Assuming a tour guide doesn't pilot me around the grit, I'm confronted by how little I know about how to navigate living and speaking in another culture.

That jolt into the unknown is invigorating when the trip is short—a vacation, a semester abroad—but when months stretch into years, when foreignness becomes a way of life, it can be deeply disorienting. The disorientation is on a psychic level as much as a physical one—I lose a sense of who I am.

I've heard this disorientation described as culture shock, a characterization that strikes me as badly misleading. Shock implies something that happens suddenly and then passes. Think, for instance, of the shock of cold you get from jumping into a frozen sea. No Polar Bear club stays in the frigid water for long. They get out, dry off, and sip cocoa by a roaring fire. They get warm; they get comfortable again. Cross-cultural living isn't like that. You can't towel off from the foreignness because it's under the skin, deep inside, an aspect of your identity that is indelible.

After living so many years outside my cultural comfort zone, I've learned to manage the strangeness of always being foreign, but the underlying feelings of dislocation don't entirely go away. I sense that I never truly belong. Even after more than a decade in Turkey, and the births of two of my children here, I often sense that I'm still a *yabancı*, a foreigner. On the days that I feel my foreignness acutely, I try to remember Abraham's story—a story that begins with a stunning blessing.

A Call and a Blessing

> Now the LORD said to Abram, "Go from your country and your kindred and your father's house to the land that I will show you. And I will make of you a great nation, and I will bless you and make your name great, so that you will be a blessing. I will bless those who bless you, and him who dishonors you I will curse, and in you all the families of the earth shall be blessed."
> So Abram went.
>
> GENESIS 12:1-4

The call and blessing of Abraham (originally called Abram) is nothing short of a new creation—the creation of a people who will walk with God, rather than away from him, a family who will be called to mediate God's blessing to all the families of the earth. Up until this point in Genesis, people had primarily chosen to go their own way, away from God and away from one another. Apart from a handful of notable exceptions, recalcitrance and rebellion had defined human relationship with God. The consequence was that violence and brutality multiplied on earth.

But then we're introduced to Abram. We're not told much about him, apart from the fact that he's a seventy-five-year-old man from Mesopotamia with a barren wife named Sarai and no son of his own. In the culture of the time, a man with no sons was a man with no future. But the voice of the Lord broke into Abram's hopeless reality with an almost unbelievable promise.

Notice, though, that the promise was preceded by a call. A future of living in God's blessing was predicated on a leaving.

With a stark imperative command, God said, "Go." The destination is left obscure. Abram is told that God will reveal where he's headed once he pulls up the tent pegs and sets off in the direction of "the land that I will show you." That's not exactly the level of detail I would want before deciding to move internationally. But that's all Abram gets, because the call is not primarily about the destination; it's about the company. God asks him to walk away from the known into the unknown *with him*. The focus of the call is not about where Abram is going so much as it is about walking alongside the one who leads the way.

God may be obscure about Abram's destination, but he's crystal clear about all that Abram will leave behind: *your country*, *your kindred*, and *your father's house*. Go from the villages, fields, valleys, and paths that you know like the back of your hand. Go from the place where everyone speaks your language and laughs at your jokes. Go from the community of people who have known you all your life. Go from the warmth of the home where there is always a place for you at the table. Tear yourself from the social fabric that made you who you are. This terrifying departure means leaving the "presumed world of norms and security" far behind.[1]

God asks Abram to leave his *country, kindred,* and *father's house*—in this progression, the circle of relations grows ever closer so that we're meant to feel the demand of the call. The Hebrew word translated "kindred" indicates a social group like a clan. But the phrase for "father's house" conveys the closest and most precious relationships.[2] These are the relationships that form character. God's call to Abram is fundamentally a call to leave an *identity.* Culture, heart language, national identity, shared history, community, friends, family, home—together, these all mingle in mysterious ways to give us our sense of self. We identify with them and we're identified by them. God is asking Abram to let go of this culturally and socially constructed identity in order to find his true identity in him.

The demand of this call is not just directed toward Abram. It's directed to each one of us.

Pilgrims on the Way Home

Since the genesis of Christianity, Abram (later renamed Abraham) has been considered a paradigm—an example of faith to be imitated, a point made clear in passages like Romans 4 and Hebrews 11:8-19. Early Christian communities understood that God's call to Abraham had a claim on their lives. In the sixth century, Saint Columba, an Irish monk driven by a desire to see the pagan Picts come to faith, challenged his brothers to follow in Abraham's footsteps. He taught that Abraham's obedience "is incumbent on all the faithful; that is to leave their country and their land, their wealth and their worldly delight for the sake of the Lord of the Elements, and go in perfect pilgrimage in imitation of Him."[3]

Historian Esther de Waal explains that in the Celtic understanding, pilgrimage did not mean a journey to Jerusalem or to a particular holy site. Instead, Celtic Christians thought of pilgrimage as *peregrinatio*, a concept inspired by Abraham's experience. It meant to go not knowing exactly where you were headed, not knowing if you would ever return. It meant to go with God, trusting in his protective presence and guiding direction.[4] It touches on the essential truth that the Christian experience is a homeless existence because ultimately, we must find our home in Christ: "For you died," says the apostle Paul, "and your life is now hidden with Christ in God" (Colossians 3:3, NIV).

Jesus' call echoes the directness of God's call to Abram—it is a call to follow without a disclosure of the destination. When Jesus met Peter, James, and John on Lake of Gennesaret's shore and called them to follow, they immediately dropped their nets and left their boats. They "left *everything*," Luke says, "and followed him" (Luke 5:11, NIV, emphasis added). Levi the tax collector responded to the call to follow with the same wholehearted obedience: "Leaving *everything*, he rose and followed him" (Luke 5:28, emphasis added). Somehow these men sensed that being in the presence of a carpenter from Galilee was worth leaving *everything*—their livelihood, their families, their plans for the future. They left to be with Jesus and to find themselves in him.

Later, when Jesus was speaking to the crowds gathered around him, he was explicit about the demands of following him: "Any one of you who does not renounce *all that he has* cannot be my disciple" (Luke 14:33, emphasis added).[5] When I hear these words, a wave of anxiety rushes through me, and I think, *I could never do that.* I don't have the strength to be like Abraham, like James, like John, like Levi, like Columba. *All* that I have, *all* that is dearest—I can never give that much. If I don't feel angst at such an all-embracing mandate, then I haven't really heard what Jesus is saying.

The leaving that God asks of Abram and the renunciation that Jesus mentions both have to do with letting go. The call to let go exposes where my loyalty lies—with possessions, my national identity, my social circles, my comfort zone, or with Jesus. Country, kindred, my father's house—all these have been a profound blessing to me, but if God asks, I must willingly let them go and leave them behind. If I cling to them, tightening my grip, then they begin to possess me, and I'm no longer free to live given to God. The call to let go is a threshold leading into the exhilarating freedom to follow.

For me, letting go has meant living in rented spaces, waking up and looking through bars on my bedroom windows to see pavement and parked cars where I'd rather see a garden. It has meant letting go of the hope of raising my kids in a house with a yard. It has meant too many good-byes to count. It has meant missing my grandmother's funeral, the births of nieces and nephews, birthdays, Christmases, pretty much any family celebration you can name.

When I was young and adventurous, I didn't feel the leaving so much. I loved to fly. Travel seemed like a grand adventure. My roving spirit was invigorated by the new: new culture, new language, new faces, new pad. Then I had kids. Suddenly I felt a strong desire to settle, to nest, to put down roots. But my natural urge to nest has been consistently frustrated. When my first daughter was only two months old and her colic was at its worst, we were packing to move from Cyprus to Turkey. Then, when my son was six months old, we packed again and moved to Vancouver, Canada, living out of suitcases for a year in an eight-hundred-square-foot student apartment. Each move was precipitated by a sense of God's call, so we tried to let go and follow.

You might think that I did what was required, because when God called, we moved. But I know the truth: There are still too many days I fall far short of total obedience, too many weeks I find myself longing for a life different from the one I'm living. I long to settle into a place of belonging. On those days, I know that even though I may have physically moved, my heart hasn't let go.

Simon Weil observes that sin "is a turning of our gaze in the wrong direction."[6] When I gaze at the people and dreams I've left, rather than focusing on what God is calling me toward, then I'm looking in the wrong direction. If I gaze at the life I might have chosen for myself rather than fixing my eyes on God, then I'm looking in the wrong direction. I have to keep asking myself: Where is my gaze? Am I looking backward or forward? Am I looking at the leaving or toward the blessing?

Looking back is not always wrong. There are times when

it's essential to look back and reflect on God's goodness in the past, to observe the way his hand has guided, to understand his providence in a way you can't amid transition. Looking back to understand and worship is miles apart from looking back with regret, wishing my path had been different. Regret and discontent stop me in my tracks. But looking back to celebrate God's faithfulness nourishes my confidence and inspires me to move forward. Still, the "backward look of gratitude is not designed by God as the primary empowerment of obedience"; it is focusing on *future grace* that keeps us moving forward.[7] With God, the momentum is always forward.

Blessing for All Families on Earth

God's blessing of Abram is composed of six perfectly balanced promises that lead up to the climax of the final line:

> I will make of you a great nation,
>> and I will bless you
>> and make your name great,
>> so that you will be a blessing.
> I will bless those who bless you,
>> and him who dishonors you I will curse,
>> and in you all the families of the earth shall be
>> blessed.

GENESIS 12:2-3

There is a beautiful balance to the structure of God's blessing to Abram that illuminates the meaning. In just two verses—Genesis 12:2-3—the word *blessing* is repeated five times (*bless, blessing, bless, bless,* and *blessed,* respectively). This is exactly the number of times we have found God blessing up to this point in Scripture, and this particular blessing to Abram and his family is repeated in Genesis exactly five times.[8] The symmetry in number—five blessings before and five blessings after—suggests that this blessing is both a focal point and a turning point.

Stroke

The stress within the promise lies at the hinge in the middle and the climax of the last line. These parallel statements reveal that God's blessing of Abram is for a much wider purpose: so that he will be a blessing to "all the families of the earth."

Up to this point, God's blessing fell within the realm of common grace, goodness showered on all humanity directly from his hand. But now, we're being introduced to blessing offered to the world through a mediator, someone appointed by God to be the conduit of his blessing to others. God's blessing will flow through a faithful man willing to leave everything most precious to him; eventually it will flow through his descendants to all the families of the earth. Previously, God's blessing was unconditional and given to all. But in Abram's case, God's blessing was conditioned on obedience to a call, and it was entrusted to him for the sake of others.

There are three implications of God's promise to Abram that give us insight into the nature of blessing—*provision, protection,* and *presence.*[9]

For a man with a barren wife, God's promise to make him into "a great nation" had immediate significance—it meant that God was going to *provide him an heir*—a child of his own. One man could not grow into a great nation without children, so initially, Abram would have seen in these words the hope of having a son through whom the promise would be realized. The blessing of fertility is perfectly consistent with the blessing to Adam and Eve that we discussed in the last chapter—God is promising Abram that he, too, will be fruitful and multiply. The Creator who spoke life into being out of nothing will now demonstrate that he can create life within a barren womb.

God's blessing also serves as a shield of *protection* around Abram: "I will bless those who bless you, and *him* who dishonors you I will curse." In this verse, there is a shift from plural to singular that is often difficult to pick up on from reading an English translation. God resolves to bless "those who bless" (plural); God will curse "him" (singular) who curses.[10] God will see to it that a few cannot rob the many of this blessing.

Through faith, protection is an aspect of God's blessing that we share. The psalmist envisions God's blessing as a shield: "For you bless the righteous, O LORD; you cover him with favor as with a shield" (Psalm 5:12). And Jesus compares himself to a good shepherd who protects his sheep: "My sheep hear my voice, and I know them, and they follow me. I give them eternal life, and they will never perish, and no one will snatch them out of my hand. My Father, who has given them to me, is greater than all, and no one is able to snatch them out of the Father's hand" (John 10:27-29). In Jesus' teaching, the *hand* of God is a powerful symbol of his abiding presence and power to protect those who follow him. I've often rested in this image of my entire being—body and soul—being sheltered in God's hand.

God's *presence* is the ultimate blessing, the wellspring from which all other blessings flow. In Genesis 12, the blessing of presence is implicit in God's promise of provision and protection; but when God reiterates the blessing to Abraham's son Isaac, he makes the blessing of his presence explicit, saying, "Sojourn in this land, and *I will be with you* and will bless you" (Genesis 26:3, emphasis added). Again, when Jacob, Abraham's grandson, dreams of a stairway tying together heaven and earth, God speaks, saying, "Behold, *I am with you* and will keep you wherever you go, and will bring you back to this land. For *I will not leave you* until I have done what I have promised you" (Genesis 28:15, emphasis added).

God with you. God with me. God with us. That's *Emmanuel*—the God who draws so near he walks among us. Living in the blessing of God's presence means recognizing that God's goodness is the atmosphere surrounding us. His mercy is the oxygen we breathe. I know an atmosphere of grace may seem intangible, but in my experience, sometimes God's presence becomes shockingly concrete.

Sheltered in God's Hand

The summer I lived alone in Bratislava, the tram incident was only the first of many terrible mishaps. The worst among them was the moment I impaled my leg on a rusty radiator screw. I passed out from the pain and ended up in an ER where a surgeon cleaned the puncture wound without anesthesia. It was 1994, and the Berlin Wall had fallen a few years earlier. Slovakia's medical system was still socialized, and hospitals were run on a shoestring budget. Supplies were severely limited. Doctors subsisted on meager state salaries, and there was no system in place to pay the kind nurses who cleaned my wound and changed the dressings every day for nearly a month. I bought them chocolate and English Breakfast tea as an expression of thanks for their care. Through it all, the blessing of God's presence sheltered me.

I had gone to Bratislava to research the relationship between art and cultural identity. One of the artists I spoke with was a bear of a man with a chestnut-colored beard. When he opened the door of his studio, which doubled as his living space, I had a strange urge to hug him, an impulse I thankfully suppressed. His apartment building was indistinguishable from every other building in the development, save for the number over the main entrance. From the standpoint of urban design, it was the imposition of the worst sort of mediocrity—a study in crushing sameness. It was in this environment that he was creating inspired paintings, their surfaces infused with subdued light.

One painting in particular stayed with me because the mood it captured crystalized my experience that summer. In the middle of an expansive field of gray green, a child sat with legs pulled tightly into his chest, arms wrapped around them in a protective gesture. The figure was simply drawn, only a contour line that read as fragile, but intact, like the permeable membrane surrounding a cell. The figure was alone but didn't appear frightened. He seemed suspended in the air, surrounded and supported by light. It is as if he were held in the arms of the atmosphere itself. That's how it feels to travel with the blessing of God's presence and protection—sheltered in a safeguarding net, held aloft by love. Psalm 139 encapsulates this reality perfectly:

> Where can I go from your Spirit?
>   Where can I flee from your presence?
> If I go up to the heavens, you are there;
>   if I make my bed in the depths, you are there.
> If I rise on the wings of the dawn,
>   if I settle on the far side of the sea,
> even there your hand will guide me,
>   your right hand will hold me fast.
>
> PSALM 139:7-10, NIV

I may live as a pilgrim in search of an eternal home, but I'll never end up on the far side of the sea alone. The voice that called me out is one with the hand that guides me. God's hand not only guides, it wraps around me, holding me fast, cradling me safe, and carrying me home.

The Gospel Beforehand

John Calvin's paraphrase of the call of Abram reads, "I command thee to go forth *with closed eyes* . . . until, having renounced thy country, thou shalt have given thyself wholly to me."[11] Perhaps Abram's eyes were closed when it came to looking back, but his eyes were wide open when it came to looking forward. Hebrews 11:9-10 tells us that "he made his home in the promised land like a stranger in a foreign country. . . . For *he was looking forward* to the city with foundations, whose architect and builder is God" (NIV, emphasis added). Abram obeyed by *faith*, looking *forward*, his eyes fixed on a promise yet to come. Even Canaan seemed to him a foreign land, because his ultimate destination was an eternal home. Those who walk in the footsteps of Abram embrace their identity as strangers and exiles on earth, "for people who speak thus make it clear that they are seeking a homeland. . . . They desire a better country, that is, a heavenly one. Therefore God is not ashamed to be called their God, for he has prepared for them a city" (Hebrews 11:14-16).

Up to God's blessing of Abram in Genesis 12, the verb "to bless" had been used multiple times, but this is the first appearance of the word used as a noun: "so that you will be *a blessing*." The Hebrew noun *berakah*, most often translated as blessing, can also mean a gift or a treaty of peace.[12] Considered that way, through Abraham, a gift—*a treaty of peace*—was being offered to the nations. The gleam of the gospel flickers in these words.[13] Paul says that by faith, "we have *peace with God* through our Lord Jesus Christ" (Romans 5:1, emphasis added). We might think of the call and blessing of Abraham as a "sneak preview for the rest of the Bible . . . Abraham as a blessing bearer of salvation is an anticipation of the blessing-bearing Christ."[14]

Paul calls God's blessing of Abraham a *protevangelion*, a Greek word that means "the gospel beforehand."[15] He explains, "The Scripture, foreseeing that God would justify the Gentiles by faith, preached *the gospel beforehand* [*protevangelion*] to Abraham, saying, 'In you shall all the nations be blessed.' So then, those who are of faith are blessed along with Abraham, the man of faith" (Galatians 3:8-9, emphasis added). The idea here is that Abraham's family tree is not purely biological in nature. *By faith,* anyone can share in the blessing of Abraham, because *by faith,* anyone can be grafted into Abraham's family.

The blessing of Abraham anticipates the gospel in its global scope. It transcends a particular clan, reaching across ethnic and racial divisions and prejudicial barriers. It is for anyone who, like Abraham, believes that God will accomplish what he has promised. We draw near to God through the same faith that invited Abraham into God's confidence. By faith, the blessing falls on us, too.

But if we partake of the blessing, then we also assume the responsibility to become blessing—to be blessing bearers to the families of the earth.

Letting Go

God's call to Abram to leave Harran was not the last time God asked him to let go of something precious. Years later, God called again, directing him to take Isaac—his son, *his only son, the son whom he loved*—on a trek to Moriah and to sacrifice him on a mountain there as an offering. God asked Abraham, the man who had waited faithfully his entire long life for the blessing of a son, to lay that blessing on an altar. The question at the heart of this excruciating test of faith recounted in Genesis 22:1-18 is whether Abraham will hold on to his greatest blessing or hold on to God. Does Isaac the blessing belong to Abraham or to God?

The moment Abraham lets go, the angel reveals a ram caught in a thicket—a sacrifice to offer in place of his son. As the ash smolders on the altar, the angel blesses Abraham, because he didn't withhold his greatest blessing.

Istanbul is not a city that wakes up early. And I'm glad, because some of my best memories here are just after dawn, when the streets are near deserted and a meditative quiet rests over our neighborhood. For two years, I walked hand-in-hand with my oldest daughter to her preschool every morning. After ducking into our favorite bakery on the way for a warm cheese croissant, we'd stroll through side streets reciting bits of Psalm 37:

> The LORD directs the steps of the godly.
> He delights in every detail of their lives.
> Though they stumble, they will never fall,
> *for the LORD holds them by the hand.*
>
> PSALM 37:23-24, NLT, EMPHASIS ADDED

I always savored that phrase while feeling the gentle pressure of my daughter's hand in mine. I'll hold on to this blessing of her presence as long as I'm able, but I know the day will come when I'll have to let her go. And when I do, I want her to go sensing that the "entire atmosphere of God's reality" goes with her.[16]

Those quiet mornings, meanwhile, feel distant now. With three kids in the house, strolling has been replaced by rushing. Spoons clatter on ceramic cereal bowls; a juice cup tips, leaving a sticky puddle on the floor. The littlest grasps my pajama leg, tugging urgently, demanding my attention. I toss a juice box into a lunchbox, calling down the hall, "Peanut butter and jelly or turkey sandwich for lunch?"

Hustle. Bustle. Clothes on. Hair brushed. Socks before boots. Sign this. Check that. Don't forget to grab your homework folder from the coffee table. When in the din of the morning rush is there a moment to stop and acknowledge together that today and every day we are resting in God's hand?

I realized that we were missing it. We were missing the moment to give the day to God.

There's a popular Irish blessing, associated with Saint Patrick, that emphasizes the protective presence of God. It's beautiful, but long—too long to say over a child dashing to catch a bus at 7:00 a.m. So I hemmed it a bit, trimming it down, making it my own.

Pausing for a moment at the open door, I pull my daughter toward me, placing my hand on her smooth hair, letting my chin rest on the top of her head. I murmur a blessing. I've prayed this prayer over my kids so many times now, they know the words by heart. As I pray she relaxes, takes a deep breath, and steps out into the world.

May the Lord go before you,
May he guard behind you,
May he walk beside you all along the way,
May his love live inside you all through the day.

chapter 3

BLESSING A CHILD

ENVISIONING FUTURE HOPE

May you grow up to be righteous
May you grow up to be true
May you always know the truth
And see the lights surrounding you . . .

BOB DYLAN, "FOREVER YOUNG,"
WRITTEN FOR HIS SON, 1974

When my grandparents stepped into the studio, they looked out of place. My grandmother was elegant in a red silk blouse and pencil skirt. Her low heels tapped on the concrete floor. My grandfather, in pressed slacks and a crisp button-down, glanced around at the paint-splattered palettes and canvases stacked against the walls. If they were scandalized by the massive paintings of lingerie by one of my studiomates or the shredded and woven canvases of another, they didn't show it. They had, after all, come with a purpose. They had come to sit for me, their oldest granddaughter, so I could paint their portrait.

For hours, they posed while I gazed and painted. Looking at someone with such concentrated attention is normally considered rude and invasive, but one of the things I love about painting portraits is that I am implicitly given permission to look intently, searchingly, intimately. I want to see beyond exterior surface to an interior world. I was trying to see something of my grandparents that I had never seen.

My grandparents had a traditional marriage. My grandfather worked full-time as an engineer while my grandmother, who had trained as a nurse during World War II, worked full-time at home caring for three children. It seemed odd that for my painting, my grandfather sat in a chair with his legs crossed, his hands folded on his knees, his expression solemn. My Gran stood behind him, her hands resting protectively on his shoulders. She glanced down, all her attention focused on Pops.

If you had known my grandparents, this is not the way you'd have expected to see them portrayed. Pops was rarely melancholy—he laughed easily and loved company and family. He was a hard worker, a man of action, not of contemplation.

But that day he seemed strangely detached, preoccupied by something coming in the distance. Gran was not normally so still, so pensive, as she was in the studio that day. She was the sort of woman who bloomed when the house was full.

None of us knew, then, that my grandfather was dying.

The following week, I painted a translucent white veil over the entire painting. When the paint was barely dry, I learned that my grandfather had been diagnosed with stomach cancer. He never recovered from the surgery to remove it. He was gone in less than two months.

My grandmother still has the painting I made of them that day. Every time I see the portrait, I think how incongruous the image is relative to most of my memories of them—it should have been more buoyant, more lively. But in those hours of attentive looking, I was able to see something I never would have noticed in a causal glance: The portrait foreshadowed the loss we were about to experience as a family. My grandfather's intuitive sense of the gathering storm. My grandmother's protective gesture, her gentle hold a sign of her longing to shelter him and keep him with her as long as possible. My grandfather was about to leave, and none of us were ready to see him go. The painting became a record of a moment when looking became seeing and seeing became vision.

Focused Attention: The First Step to Blessing

Blessing begins with seeing. Before words of blessing can reach toward future vision, we must attend to present reality. And that means we must turn our gaze from ourselves—our issues, anxieties, and preoccupations—and see others as they long to be seen. This is *agape seeing*, a way of seeing grounded in love and sacrifice. It takes time and discernment, inviting God to help us truly see.

The idea that blessing requires seeing another may sound so obvious that it hardly seems worth noting. But in truth, I'm finding this one of the most difficult aspects of blessing for two reasons: First, it goes against the grain of my natural tendency to focus primarily on myself, my needs, my wants, my interests. Second, it requires me to free myself from the distractions of modern life to carve out time to look at and listen to others with focused attention.

No one craves attention more than children. Their souls aren't guarded, but they aren't right on the surface, either. It takes time to uncover them, to begin to sense their hopes, longings, and potential. Kids are needy, for sure, and a lot of their need is simply to be seen and blessed through the seeing.

Lately, I've been busy with a new job, working odd hours, often from home. I know I've been a distracted mom. My kids walk in from school, drop their backpacks on the ground, but my gaze stays intent on my computer screen.

I've been so absorbed in my virtual work, virtual relationships, virtual reality that I didn't even notice, but apparently someone has been trying to get my attention. I feel my daughter's small hands on my cheeks. She takes my face firmly in her grip, prying my eyes away from the computer screen. Gravely and insistently, in a voice too mature for her four years, she says, "Mom, look at me . . . look at me *in the eyes*."

She knows when I'm not seeing her. She perceives that I'm not even trying to look.

In a time when my attention is constantly pulled in so many directions, when screens and pings and tweets and posts and whatever happens to be trending at the moment demand my attention, it's hard to truly see. It's so much easier to be absorbed by digital noise without realizing how blinded I've become to the inner lives of those near, those who share my home and sit around my table. Meaning is veiled by distraction. The fragmentation of my attention keeps me from seeing with insight the people who are closest. When my consciousness frays around the edges, distraction keeps me from seeing with the sort of clarity of vision that's essential to blessing.

I've been meditating on two stories in Genesis that touch on the relationship between vision and blessing. Both stories involve children being blessed by their fathers—both men blinded by age. One couldn't see for blindness, the other could see in spite of blindness. One man's name was Isaac; the other was his son Jacob.

Isaac was the son of Abraham, the recipient of the promise that all the families of the earth would be blessed through him. God himself bestowed the blessing first given to the father on the son, demonstrating that blessing is intended to move from generation to generation, always multiplying and expanding, like the branches of a tree reaching to the heavens (Genesis 26:1-5). God blessed Abraham and Isaac directly, but Isaac and his son Jacob mediate God's blessing to their children. The family that God blessed begins to speak blessing to each other, but when the first blessing is spoken from father to son, it doesn't have the salutary effect I expect.

Instead of drawing the family together, the blessing invokes a murderous rage that nearly rips the family apart.

When a Blessing Goes Wrong: What Not to Do

In the culture of the time, the father was expected to bless the oldest son with both material and spiritual inheritance. The birthright (*bekorah*) referred to the gift of property—land and livestock—and the largest share of wealth. The blessing (*berakah*) came from the father's soul and inspired vitality, strength, and leadership.[1] From a social, economic, and religious perspective, the birthright and the blessing together made the oldest son the primary carrier of a family's heritage. In the line of Abraham, that heritage had been shaped by God and included a future blessing with global reach.

Esau, Isaac's oldest son, had already foolishly given away his birthright to his younger brother, Jacob, surrendering the blessing of property and wealth that was rightly his. Now all that was left was his father's spoken blessing—*the blessing of the soul*. When Isaac prepared to bestow his blessing on his oldest son, Esau, he "was old and his eyes were dim *so that he could not see*" (Genesis 27:1, emphasis added). Isaac's lack of vision set the stage for an elaborate deception that poisoned the blessing.

Isaac summoned Esau and asked him to go out hunting and prepare a delicious meal so that "*my soul may bless you before I die*" (Genesis 27:4, emphasis added). Esau rushed to fulfill his father's desire: A spoken blessing from the soul was far more treasured than property and livestock that came with the birthright because, as the source of abundant life, it was infinitely renewable.

Meanwhile, Jacob, encouraged by his mother, Rebekah, was conspiring to steal Esau's blessing. Jacob wrapped himself in his brother's musky robe and covered his smooth hands and neck in goatskin. His costume might have been comical in its extreme clumsiness, but it did the job because his father *couldn't see.*

Isaac's physical blindness might have been symptomatic of willful spiritual blindness. At the birth of the brothers, the Lord revealed that the older would serve the younger—Jacob would be preeminent over Esau (Genesis 25:23). Assuming Isaac knew the prophecy but secretly sought to upend the Lord's will by blessing Esau while excluding Jacob, his move was an attempt to circumvent God's good plan for his family. Jacob's scheming, on the other hand, was a desperate and misguided grab to attain the blessing he feared his father would withhold. The actions of father, mother, and sons are stained by deceit. Although neither secrecy nor scheming could frustrate God's will for this beloved family, underhanded manipulative actions had consequences—they eroded trust and tore the family apart.

Esau returned from the hunt to learn the treasured blessing had been bestowed on his brother. He wept bitterly for the blessing he had lost, and then despair hardened into rage: Esau wanted to kill his brother.

A parent's blessing should strengthen a family's character, not fracture it. This story pivots on the assumption that a word spoken from one generation to another is truly efficacious, that it has a real, substantial effect in shaping the lives of children.[2] The content of Isaac's blessing might have been good, even reflecting God's will for the whole family. But the way in which it was given—secretly, stealthily, exclusively—ruined a blessing that could have helped both sons flourish. Isaac and Rebekah's covert attempts to elevate one child over another are a reminder that we can never underestimate the power of sin in our lives to corrupt even our best attempts at parenting. A blessing that becomes a tool to achieve our own ends is no blessing at all.

Favoritism is a subtle poison that embitters one child against another. Jealousy and sibling rivalry sprout up easily enough; we certainly don't want to cultivate them by sowing seeds of discord, blessing one child to the exclusion of another. It occurs to me that the vision required to bless well includes willingness to search my heart and examine my motivations. Am I driven by my own agenda and ambition for my children, or are my blessings shaped by the Lord? Do my words impose my own vision, or free my kids to live in God's grace? Am I using blessing as a manipulative tool, or offering it as gift?

I turn to Genesis 48 and 49—Jacob's blessing of his grandchildren and children—looking to understand some of the secrets of crafting blessings that express future hope and include God-given vision. The blessings in these chapters provide a primer in elements that can be integrated into any blessing.

Vision That Inspires Blessing

When Jacob's son Joseph heard that his father was about to die, he brought his two sons, Manasseh and Ephraim, to receive a blessing. As soon as Jacob asked for the boys to be brought near, "that I may bless them," we're told: "Now the eyes of Israel were dim with age, so that *he could not see*" (Genesis 48:9-10, emphasis added). This description perfectly echoes the description of Isaac we read earlier. Jacob was blind. Just like his father, Isaac, his eyesight degenerated with age. This critical detail invites us to read these two blessing events side by side: Will Jacob's blessing fracture the family or strengthen it? Will his children and grandchildren be divided by rivalry or unified in faith?

The moment Jacob embraced Joseph, he confessed, "I never expected to see your face; and behold, *God has let me see* your offspring also" (Genesis 48:11, emphasis added).

"*God has let me see . . .*": Jacob might have been physically blind, but his spiritual vision was a God-given gift, born of a long night of wrestling for a blessing (but that's another story we'll get to later). God enabled Jacob to see the boys, not with his degenerating eyesight, but with the eyes of his soul. He saw their value and their identity in relationship to the God who had led and redeemed him. Seeing in this way is a gift that translates into blessing. We don't muster this kind of vision in our own strength. It grows out of a relationship with God and is nurtured by prayer, worship, struggle, and trust.

Notice that when Jacob rested his hands on the young men and blessed them, his opening words focused on the character of the God he'd come to know through lived experience:

> The God before whom my fathers Abraham and Isaac
> walked,
>   the God who has been my shepherd all my life long
>   to this day,

> the angel who has redeemed me from all evil, bless the
>   boys;
> and in them let my name be carried on, and the
>   name of my fathers Abraham and Isaac;
> and let them grow into a multitude in the midst of
>   the earth.

GENESIS 48:15-16

Jacob's blessing of his grandchildren begins with a statement about God's identity, reminding his grandsons that God has revealed himself to their family over the generations. And his blessing incorporates his own personal experience with God—"the God who has been *my shepherd* all my life long" (emphasis added). It's worth noting that this is the first time in Scripture that God has been described as a shepherd. Jacob, a skilled shepherd who had cared for his uncle's flocks for nearly two decades,[3] invites the boys to experience God as part of a family shepherded by the Lord.

Jacob's understanding of God is more fully expressed later, in his blessing of his son Joseph. In that blessing, Jacob uses no less than five names for God, all deeply personal, alluding to the experiences that had transformed him from Jacob (the deceiver) into Israel (the one who struggles with God and prevails).[4] He calls God "the Mighty One of Jacob," "the Shepherd," "the Stone of Israel," "the God of your father," "the Almighty" (Genesis 49:24-25). Three of the five names directly refer to Jacob's own relationship with the Lord—the God of his forefathers has become his own God. The greatest blessing any child can receive is a parent who walks with God, experiencing his presence personally in a transforming way.

Hebrews 11:21 says that as Jacob blessed the boys, he was "bowing in worship." Blessing and worship spring from the same source—a vision of God's good character and a heart full of trust in God's promises. Worship is an irrepressible response to seeing who God is in his glory and to rightly perceiving that the blessings that populate our lives are expressions of his grace.

When Isaac, in his blindness, blessed Jacob, he began by observing qualities he loved about his son: "The smell of my son is like the smell of a field that the LORD has blessed" (Genesis 27:27, NIV). In stark contrast, Jacob's blessing of Ephraim and Manasseh starts with qualities Jacob loves about God—his faithfulness to the generations, his protective presence as a watchful shepherd, his redemptive power. Jacob's blessing is inspired by recognition of how dependent he's been on God over the years for his own spiritual formation. Blessing blends with worship because both are expressed *with* the Lord. His presence should be felt in the blessing.

"A home is a subtle, implicit laboratory of spirit . . ." suggests John O'Donohue, "quietly shaping belief, expectation, and life direction. Parents are invisible creators."[5] Our attention or inattention, care or indifference, seeing or blindness, blessing or negativity—they all have an inestimable impact on the spiritual landscape of the children in our care. The blessing of our children can't be separated from the vitality of our own relationship with God. Blessing begins with seeing both our children *and* the God who blesses us.

What Do You Think I'll Be When I Grow Up?

There's a light on at the end of the hallway. I shuffle down and peer into my oldest daughter's room. A pool of light spilling out from under an embroidered lampshade falls on the pages of the book in her hand. Her form is lost, snug under a voluminous duvet. I sit on the edge of the bed, resting my hand somewhere near her knee. She's sleepy, but she has a question for me: "What do you think I'll be when I grow up?"

I don't answer right away. I'm too tired to think deep and answer well. The first response that springs to mind is honest: "I don't know." But it sounds lame and uninspiring. Even as it flashes through my mind, I sense the inadequacy. It's not enough. It's not the answer she needs from me.

I don't want to dismiss her query, so I try to hear the question behind the question. What is she really asking?

I realize she's asking if I see her. She's asking what qualities and strengths I see *in her* and how I envision those developing in her life.

Answering her question with discernment requires me to look not at her, but *into her*, and even beyond her, to identify qualities that may now only be in their infancy but could be developed to become a force for good in her life and in the lives of others. And most importantly, answering the question well requires spiritual vision, because even when I look with all the intensity I can muster, I might miss something that God may be preparing her for if the eyes of my heart aren't wide open. If I see her with vision, and then find a way to express what the Lord reveals, then my answer becomes blessing.

Oh Lord, I am inadequate for this. I cannot see the way I need to see to bless well, but I long to see, even as I long to be seen.

I begin to pray for insight into answering my daughter's question. Her birthday is on the horizon. She's nearly twelve, just on the cusp of adolescence. This year, I've watched as her limbs lengthened. I've noticed as she's withdrawn into her interior space, wondering about what all these changes mean. She's standing on a threshold, moving from one season of life into another.

When Jacob blessed Ephraim and Manasseh, they weren't young children. The Hebrew word within the blessing sometimes translated "boys" or "lads" (Genesis 48:16) indicates young men of marriageable age. These young men were at a pivotal time in their lives. Hovering on the cusp of adulthood, their futures had not yet been set. They were just at the age when their decisions would have enduring consequences. What more essential time to be affirmed, valued, and reminded that God is a shepherd who leads and redeems?

My girl, since the first moment I held her, has illuminated my days. Now it's my responsibility to invite her soul to growth. Not just any blessing will do. I need to write a blessing that's *suitable* to her. (I'll do the same for each of my three children.)[6] To mark this special occasion in her life, I want to compose a blessing that shows her that she's been seen and that she's been loved through the seeing.

I go away for a weekend with a friend, and there's really only one agenda for this quiet retreat—to write a blessing for my daughter. I want to help lift her into this new season with words that encapsulate the qualities I've seen in her and the good I believe God wills for her. Searching for inspiration, I turn to the blessings Jacob gave to each of his twelve sons.

Crafting a Suitable Blessing

We've already identified focused attention and encounter with God as fundamental aspects of blessing. Blessing may begin with seeing, but in the end, the seeing must be expressed in words. "A blessing fulfills its purpose *only when it is actually verbalized*," suggest John Trent and Gary Smalley. Drawing on years of counseling experience, they believe blessings should be "spoken in person, written down, or preferably both. For a child in search of the blessing, silence communicates mostly confusion."[7]

Jacob's blessing of Ephraim and Manasseh is a prelude to his blessing of each of his twelve sons with "a blessing suitable for them" (Genesis 49:28, isv). Genesis 49 does not represent an off-the-cuff speech. Jacob's words were carefully composed so that they would be remembered and recited because a nation was being founded—the nation of Israel. And while no blessing we ever give will carry this degree of gravity, this passage reminds us that some of the most meaningful blessings are not general or spontaneous; they're composed with particular recipients in mind.

There's so much that's strange to me about these blessings. In fact, some of them don't strike me as blessings at all. But three principles are beginning to take shape that are helping me craft a blessing for my girl.

First, Jacob incorporates evocative metaphors that *activate the imagination*. Creative vision is laced all through Jacob's blessing of his sons: Judah is a crouching lion. Issachar is a protective "strong donkey." Dan is a lethal "viper by the path." Joseph is "a fruitful bough by a spring." Benjamin is "a ravenous wolf." I admit that it would *never* occur to me to compare one of my kids to a donkey, a viper, or a wolf. None of those metaphors communicate virtues to me. But it's likely that at the time, these images conveyed strength, power, and vitality.[8]

Cultural distance aside, these visual metaphors stimulate our imaginations by painting pictures in our minds, etching the imagery into memory. The language Jacob uses to describe Judah, for instance, is regal. He prophecies that "the scepter shall not depart from Judah" (Genesis 49:10), alluding to the reality that a line of kings will emerge from this tribe. Beginning with David, we can follow the royal line born of Judah all the way to Jesus, who is described in Revelation as the triumphant "Lion of the tribe of Judah" (Revelation 5:5).

Images can be revelatory. Visual imagery expressed through poetic language has an emotive force that speaks powerfully to some aspects of truth in a way that precise technical terminology never can. Perhaps that is why we find it so often in Jesus' teaching. Jesus was the master of the metaphor. His teaching conjures up images of fertile fields ripe for harvest, fruitful vineyards, mustard seeds that grow into majestic trees, priceless pearls, young women waiting in the dark with flickering lamps, wayward sheep, and a welcoming father embracing a lost son. These suggestive metaphors drawn from everyday life communicate deep theological content about the nature of God and his Kingdom. In Eugene

Peterson's marvelous summation, "Metaphor is a word that carries us across the abyss separating the invisible from the visible."[9] Whenever I'm tempted to contrast imaginative thinking with thinking about what is real and true, I remember Mircea Eliade's insight that imagination should never imply "arbitrary invention." He explains that "to have imagination is to be able to see the world in its totality."[10]

When I was a child, a Brazilian pastor who was visiting our home blessed me. My memory of his specific phrasing is hazy, but I do remember the image he painted as he prayed over me. He prayed that I would become an oak of righteousness, a planting of the Lord—a phrase he no doubt lifted from Isaiah 61:3. When he spoke these words, I could barely have been described as a spindly sapling. Even now, there are lots of days when I feel like a scrawny shrub, fruitless and thirsty. But the image of a thriving oak with deep roots has stayed with me over the years, implanting in my heart a desire to see the blessing realized.

This past fall, we spent a few months in a house on a quiet street in a western North Carolina town. Outside my bedroom window, a grand oak presided over the block with authority and grace. Its branches, the size of most tree trunks, supported a stunning canopy that I watched turn from green to golden and then drop crisp, brittle leaves on our lawn and driveway. Raking and bagging loads of leaves, I found countless acorns underneath. Oaks may not be fruit-bearing trees, but they are definitely seed bearing, and each of those acorns—far too many for the scores of neighborhood squirrels to steal away for the winter—had within them the promise of another tree, another life. One mighty tree produced enough acorns in one season to plant an entire forest. One tree showered life all over the neighborhood.

Second, Jacob's blessings prepare his children to face challenges even as they express future hope. The goal of blessing our children shouldn't be to insulate them from the world; it should be to fill them with the spiritual reserves to face whatever challenges they find there. Jacob's blessings don't obscure the trials he sees coming for his sons: Gad will be the victim of tribal raids, but "he shall raid at their heels" (Genesis 49:19). Joseph will be attacked and harassed by archers, but his bow will remain unmoved and his arms will be agile (Genesis 49:23-24). Both these blessings acknowledge difficulty while asking God to strengthen these men, helping them endure conflict and thrive in its wake.

When our youngest daughter was born, my husband wrote a blessing for her baby dedication. One of the phrases in an otherwise tender blessing initially struck me as too sad to pray over a newborn: "Naomi, my daughter, in this life, you may find hardship or tragedy. When you do, may you have someone as loyal and kind as Ruth to walk beside you."

When I first read those words, I recoiled, thinking, *No, I don't want her to experience tragedy. I don't want her to feel the sting of loss. That shouldn't be part of the blessing.* But as I reflected on the reality that no life is lived without loss, I realized that my husband's words were meant to pray her through pain that is inevitable in a broken world. Blessings can help our children navigate hard roads by giving them an inner compass that guides even through crisis and disappointment.

Finally, Jacob's blessings are grounded in truth. He affirms his sons' strengths; he also identifies areas for growth.

The blessings of Reuben, Simeon, and Levi—the first three in the chapter—don't read as blessings at all. There is such a critical edge to Jacob's words to these men that the Old Testament scholar and author Bruce Waltke calls them "antiblessings."[11] Rather than affirming his sons, Jacob censures them, calling out volatility that threatened the moral and physical well-being of everyone around them.

None of Jacob's sons were saints—they all participated in selling their brother into slavery (Genesis 37:12-36). But Reuben, Simeon, and Levi's offenses were so grievous that they had to be addressed within the family: Jacob's judgment curbed their influence on succeeding generations by removing them from leadership. Jacob's antiblessings, then, might be interpreted as disciplinary words meant to protect the family as a whole. "In terms of the nation's destiny these antiblessings *are a blessing.* By demoting Reuben for his turbulence and uncontrolled sex drive, Jacob saves Israel from reckless leadership. Likewise, by cursing the cruelty of Simeon and Levi, he restricts their cruel rashness from dominating."[12] For these three adult sons, the correction is the blessing.

Blessing and cursing may be polar opposites, but edifying correction spoken within the security of family bonds finds a place within blessing. Since words of blessing always have our children's thriving in view, it's impossible to affirm behaviors that we know will devastate their bodies and spirits. Careful correction born of love is never a curse—it's a blessing, because it seeks the restoration and wholeness of a soul. When correction is clear but merciful, it can motivate character change. Look, for instance, at the spiritual development in the life of the tribe of Levi. In Jacob's blessing, Levi is disciplined for his ferocious anger. And yet generations later, when Moses blesses Levi, it's evident that the life of this tribe has been totally transformed. No longer violent, Levi has become "godly"; no longer angry, Levi has become steadfast by observing God's word and keeping the covenant (Deuteronomy 33:8-11).

Jacob's disciplinary words inspired such a dramatic character change in the life of the tribe that Moses, who was himself from the tribe of Levi, was inspired to entrust Levi with the spiritual leadership of the entire nation: "They shall teach Jacob your rules and Israel your law; they shall put incense before you and whole burnt offerings on your altar. Bless, O Lord, his substance, and accept the work of his hands" (33:10-11). A wayward son was transformed into a tribe of priests.

• • •

Back to the task at hand—composing a blessing for my daughter who is turning twelve. I want this blessing to be perfectly suited to her in the way that Jacob's blessings were suited to each of his sons. Through conceptualizing this blessing, I'm learning that blessing doesn't just amount to words written on a page. Blessing embraces the whole process of encountering God in prayer and worship, seeing and discerning nascent qualities in my daughter that could be developed, expressing blessing in words communicated to her, and committing myself to her spiritual formation while releasing her into God's hands. Ultimately, the blessing is not a vision of *what* she will be when she grows up, it's about *who* she will become. It's not about occupation, it's about character formation.

In a notebook, I jot down memories from her childhood, Scripture that has informed our prayers, challenges I imagine she'll face in the next few years, and truth I most want to affirm for her. I write and then rewrite while talking with God about my beloved little one who's not so little anymore. Over time, the blessing emerges. When the words have taken shape, I write them for her on the first few pages of a new journal.

On the morning of her birthday, we all gather in the den, relaxing after a pancake breakfast. I read the blessing, emotion making the words full in my throat, but I want her to hear me say them. The blessing—composed, prayed, and spoken—is my gift given to her.

Remember that evening when we were walking by
the water just before sunset and you coaxed a wild
bunny to eat from your hand? You knelt down in the
green lawn and waited by some blackberry bushes,
your open hand filled with some grass from the
field. You were only six, but you waited still, patient,
and gentle as the rabbit hesitantly inched in your
direction, and eventually nibbled the grass held in
your palm.

Watching you that evening, I saw so many
of the qualities we've been praying for since you
were born—love, joy, peace, patience, kindness,
gentleness, faithfulness, self-control. *May our
gardener God continue to plant and cultivate spiritual
fruit in your spirit to nourish others.*

Ever since you were young, you've had a natural sensitivity to the beauty of the world. You marveled at color, form, and light in plants and animals. *May you always retain your sense of wonder, craving beauty, truth, and goodness.*

Every day, I see you maturing in so many ways, some observable, some under the surface of your skin. Realize the people God brings into your life share in helping you become the person you're meant to be. May you be drawn to friends who delight in your particularities and encourage you to be yourself, rather than trying to shape you into their own image. The best friends see your potential and help draw it out. They never shame, never manipulate, never belittle. *May you be the friend to others that you want others to be to you.*

Over the years, you'll meet so many different sorts of people—many will act differently, think differently, believe differently, and make choices you might not understand. Even when you feel confused by the different, remember that God's image is imprinted deep within each and every one of them. *May you honor the image of God in each person by relating to others with dignity, kindness, and love.*

Every moment of every day, may you be certain of one thing: that you are loved. You are loved by me and your dad, and by God. This isn't a love you earned. It's not a love you can lose. You're loved beyond comprehension just because you were given to us and you'll always be part of the fabric of our lives.

Like the wild rabbit you fed when you were so small, may you return every evening to eat from the Lord's hand. May you meet God each day and allow him to speak truth into your inner being about your inestimable worth and your welcome around his table as a beloved daughter in Christ.

chapter 4

BLESSING THAT CREATES COMMUNITY

SEEING (AND BEING) SHINE

Oh! never till thyself reveal thy face,
Shall I be flooded with life's vital grace.
Oh make my mirror-heart thy shining-place,
And then my soul, awaking with the morn,
Shall be a waking joy, eternally new-born.

GEORGE MCDONALD, *A BOOK OF STRIFE IN THE FORM*
OF THE DIARY OF AN OLD SOUL, 1880

When I was thirteen, I had an unexpected brush with death. One evening at dinner, I slipped from consciousness. I slumped in my chair, fell sideways, and ended up sprawled on the vinyl kitchen floor, not breathing.

I don't have any memory of the panic that gripped my family in the wake of my fall. But I've been told that my two younger sisters cried in terror and my mother immediately began mouth-to-mouth resuscitation. My father must have called the paramedics, because the only hazy memory I have of the incident is feeling my mother's warm breath on my face and hearing her pleading prayers as I was lifted onto a stretcher and wheeled out of the house into the sterile interior of an ambulance.

The week before I ruined a perfectly good family dinner, I had been bundled up on the couch, feverish and listless. My mother took me to see the doctor not once, but twice. I appeared to be sick with a virus—a normal childhood illness—but my immune system never rallied to fight it. My mom was an attentive nurse, dutifully plying me with a variety of fluids from chicken broth to ginger ale, but over the course of days, I became increasingly dehydrated, and then I stopped breathing.

I spent a week in the hospital—sleeping, mostly, and being pricked here and there for a whole spectrum of tests and scans. Nothing particularly insidious ever turned up; my system, apparently, was just spent. But for a self-conscious teenager, my strange, unidentifiable illness jolted me into the realization that life doesn't go on forever.

Since the doctors weren't exactly sure what was causing

my malaise, only medical professionals and my mother were allowed into my room. Friends visited, but they were separated from me by a glass partition. I could see them peering through the glass, waving awkwardly, empathetic smiles failing to conceal anxiety. My friends were there, but they were removed from my touch. They were present, concerned, sympathetic, but they couldn't save me. The glass was a transparent chasm. Isolated and confined to a hospital bed, I remember being conscious for the first time of the solitariness of existence. For the first time, I understood that the self—*myself*—was contained behind invisible walls that others couldn't breach.

The day I was released from the hospital, there was only one place I wanted to go: the place where I had felt someone reaching through the wall into my inner self, the place where my existential sense of loneliness evaporated in the light of divine presence. I wanted to go to church.

So, before returning home, my parents drove me to church. It wasn't a Sunday, and there was no reason for anyone to be in the building. The sanctuary was hushed. I sat down on a pew, a solitary, thin teenager in a vast, modern space constructed of roughly hewn gray stone. Sunlight filtered through the stained glass. The windows—a set of six, three on either side of the pulpit—depicted scenes from the life of Christ. One of the windows showed Jesus praying in Gethsemane. He knelt in anguish, his hands clasped in petition, his eyes lifted to the heavens. A beam like a divine tether broke through the indigo sky, bathing his face in light.

There it was—*the shine*. I rested in the radiance that

unified Father and Son, illustrated in cut glass and leaded lines. I had come to church to feel that light shining on me, shining *into* me. The hospital room had been plenty light, but it had been florescent light. Artificial light is nothing like daylight. Man-made light is nothing like God's light. In the sanctuary, I felt true light. The illumination didn't come from the space itself, but it emanated from what happened in the space, from what was said and from what was sung and from the way people related to one another and from that ineffable presence that moved in the space between proclamation, worship, and fellowship.

I'm old enough to know now that not everyone's experience of church is so luminous. And I know, too, that the spiritual light isn't confined to the space of a building. It blazes in unexpected places far from the plush interior of a North American church. But when I was young, I associated light with church, and I was at church a lot because I was a pastor's kid.

My father was not the sort of pastor who carried his vocation around like a burden. I saw him in the pulpit every Sunday, and I saw him at the dinner table every night, and in both settings, he never seemed jaded or weary, just full of creativity and curiosity and, well, light. There was a vital energy in my dad's ministry and in our home that meant we were busy, but the busyness didn't feel purposeless; it felt meaningful. When I reflect on my childhood, I don't have many memories of still moments. It seems something was always happening, that we were always on the move. But there is a recurring moment that hangs in my memory like a divine pause—the benediction every Sunday. On Sunday mornings, after the hymns, the offering, the prayers, and the sermon, there was the blessing.

Along with the law given to the people of Israel at Sinai, God composed a specific blessing to be prayed over his people whenever they gathered for worship. God charged Aaron and his sons—the tribe of Levi—with speaking the blessing that became an integral, essential part of Israel's experience of God. And thousands of years after its composition, the same blessing became an integral, essential part of my experience with God, because on Sundays, I stood in the congregation as my father stood behind the pulpit, raised his right hand in a gesture that struck me as both authoritative and generous, and said,

> May the LORD bless you and keep you;
> may the LORD make His face shine on you
>   and be gracious to you;
> may the LORD look on you with favor
>   and give you peace.
> NUMBERS 6:24-26, AUTHOR'S PARAPHRASE

On Sundays when I was paying attention, the words washed over me like a tidal wave. Today, they still hit me with a force that sweeps me off my feet; I can feel the irresistible pull of the undertow drawing me back into the turbulence of divine shine. Blessing, protection, grace, peace, seeing the shining face of God and living in his favor—this is God's blessing to those who meet with him. It expresses all that we're meant to experience in worship and all that we're meant to carry with us as we walk out of the sanctuary and into the world.

When God Writes a Blessing

Just as God initiated blessing in the first chapters of Genesis, God crafted a blessing to be spoken over his people out of his own initiative. This priestly blessing wasn't reserved for special occasions. It was integrated into Israel's daily experience with God. From the moment it was first read at the foot of Mount Sinai up until the first century when Jesus went to the synagogue to pray, this blessing was an essential thread in the fabric of Israel's worship each day.[1] Even though the blessing was incorporated into what we might identify as formal liturgy, it isn't a formality. God doesn't author formalities— he authors life. And there is life in this blessing, if we're open to receiving it.

The blessing is composed of three balanced phrases (as translated in the Holman Christian Standard Bible) that encapsulate the goodness of living each day in the presence of the Lord:

> May Yahweh bless you and protect you;
> may Yahweh *make His face shine on you* and be gracious
>   to you;
> may Yahweh look with favor on you and give you
>   peace.

YHWH, YHWH, YHWH—all three phrases of the blessing begin with the name of God that is so holy, Orthodox Jews don't pronounce it out of reverence. We are meant to feel the repetition of the name that in English is translated "LORD."[2] The repetition has a way of emphasizing that the

Lord, alone, is the source of this blessing that encapsulates God's desire for those in relationship with him.

To ensure that we don't miss the vital point that this blessing is for those related to God, the blessing concludes with the clarifying statement: "So shall they [the priests] *put my name upon the people* of Israel" (Numbers 6:27, emphasis added). God is the one who extends blessing to his people, and when he blesses them, *they bear his name.*

Naming is an intimate, powerful act because it is about bestowing identity. Those who are named with God are part of his family and should bear a family resemblance. Above all, they should reflect his character. In this blessing, that means that they will become mirrors of his shine.

The first phrase of the blessing—*May Yahweh bless you and protect you*—evokes God's covenant blessing of Abraham, Isaac, and Jacob (Genesis 12:3, 26:3, 28:14-15). There's a reassuring continuity in this phrase revealing that the God who is blessing now is the same God who has blessed in the past. The continuity engenders trust by demonstrating that God is reliable and faithfully honors his promises. In the past, God had blessed those he called with provision, protection, and presence. And this blessing shows that God will continue to do the same for those who are identified by his name.

While there is continuity in the blessing, there is innovation, too. In this blessing, a new dynamic enters God's relationship with his people. The second and third lines of the blessing veer off in a thrilling trajectory. They breathe an exhilarating newness that would have challenged the Israelites' expectations of what their relationship with God would look like moving forward. The innovation in the blessing is centered in shine.

Unveiling God's Shine

The experience of living illuminated by the shining face of the Lord is the heart of the Aaronic blessing. When I recite the blessing aloud, I always linger on the verb *shine*. Whether I pronounce the blessing in a full-throated authoritative tone or barely whisper it under my breath, the emphasis naturally falls on the words "May Yahweh make His face *shine* on you." This phrase is much more than poetic metaphor, because in the context of the story of Moses' encounter with God on Mount Sinai, it touched on a visible reality.

The shine referred to in this blessing is not the shimmer of a flickering candle flame; it's more like the blaze of the sun at noon in the desert. This shine is the glory of *Yahweh's* presence—shine so intense, it's blinding. This is the shine of the pillar of fire that illuminated a path out of slavery toward freedom in the Promised Land. It is the shine that radiated out through the linen curtains and goatskin cover of the Tabernacle like a floodlight burning in the wilderness. This is the shine that lit up Mount Sinai and lingered on Moses' face when he hiked down from the peak of the mountain after God had given him the law. His skin radiated with such intensity that the people couldn't stand to look him in the eye. If they winced in the face of *reflected* shine, how would they ever stand directly in the shining face of God himself?

> When Moses came down from Mount Sinai, with
> the two tablets of the testimony in his hand as he
> came down from the mountain, Moses did not know
> that *the skin of his face shone* because he had been
> talking with God. Aaron and all the people of Israel
> saw Moses, and behold, *the skin of his face shone*, and
> they were afraid to come near him.
>
> EXODUS 34:29-30, EMPHASIS ADDED

If Moses' incandescent face had been a one-time occur-
rence confined to the slopes of Sinai, it would have been
memorable, no doubt. It would have been a singular
moment—a beautiful, bright blip on the spiritual radar that
no one would expect to recur. It would have been an exception, not an expectation. But the radiance wasn't a fleeting
flash like fireworks that explode and dazzle, then sizzle and
fade. Reading on in Exodus, we find that whenever Moses
went into the Tabernacle to speak with the Lord, he was
bathed with the shine.

> When he came out and told the people of Israel
> what he was commanded, the people of Israel would
> see the face of Moses, that the skin of Moses' face
> was shining. And Moses would put the veil over his
> face again, until he went in to speak with him.
>
> EXODUS 34:34-35

Moses put a veil over his face *again*. Again and again,
Moses veiled his face in deference to the people who couldn't
bear the intensity of divine shine. The veil obscured the

reflected glory and shielded them from the shine they weren't yet prepared to face. Since the people squinted in the light of lingering glory that eventually faded, it seems audacious to ask the Lord to shine directly on them. But that is precisely what the blessing of Numbers 6 asks: May his face shine *on you*. May the shine that you see refracted on Moses' face light you up. May you experience directly the presence that you can now barely stand to glimpse indirectly. May the transcendent God, who dwells in unapproachable light, approach you in his full radiant glory.

The blessing makes it brilliantly clear that God's desire is for all his people to see and experience his shine. At Sinai, only Moses was invited to be so near to God's radiant glory. Only Moses experienced unmediated light. Only Moses spoke directly with God (Exodus 33:11). Moses mediated God's light and word to the people. He stood between God and the nation, like a bridge between a chasm dividing the peak from the valley. But this blessing clearly communicates God's desire for *all* his people to relate to him with the same familiarity that Moses enjoyed. The blessing anticipates an intimacy with God manifest in face-to-face relationship. God gives his people a glimpse of a horizon where they will encounter his shine directly. The blessing leans toward a day when the transcendent glory of God would be seen in the face of a man.

The Shine of Transfiguration

Peter, James, and John were the first to perceive the divine shine illuminating the face of the man they had dropped their fishing nets to follow. Matthew relates the revelatory incident this way:

> After six days Jesus took with him Peter and James, and John his brother, and led them up a high mountain by themselves. And he was transfigured before them, and *his face shone like the sun*, and his clothes became *white as light*. And behold, there appeared to them Moses and Elijah, talking with him.
> MATTHEW 17:1-3, EMPHASIS ADDED

On the top of a high mountain, which tradition remembers as Mount Tabor, Jesus was *transfigured*, meaning his appearance literally changed. His face and form were altered so radically that he was almost unrecognizable. Suddenly, a flesh-and-blood man seemed to have light running through his veins. Jesus' closest friends had never seen him radiant like this. "There is no other place in the entire Bible where the curtain between the material and the invisible world is completely lifted visually, and there is no other place where the manifestation of the divinity of Christ is witnessed in such a dramatic way."[3] In the Transfiguration, the spiritual reality that had been there shimmering just under the surface broke through in gorgeous clarity. The Transfiguration was a historical manifestation of the divine glory that is ahistorical, the glory that shone before time began.

Three Gospel writers give us an account of the Transfiguration (Matthew 17:1-9; Mark 9:2-10; Luke 9:28-36). But John's Gospel interprets the event, helping us understand what it meant to behold Jesus' glory revealed.

Light is a persistent theme in John's Gospel, and it was in the moment of Transfiguration that John saw it most clearly.

If we read the prologue to the book of John with the Transfiguration in mind, it's as if John is taking us up onto the mountain so we can see the shine for ourselves:

> In the beginning was the Word, and the Word was with God, and the Word was God. . . . In him was life, and the life was *the light* of men. The light *shines* in the darkness, and the darkness has not overcome it . . .
>
> And the Word became flesh and dwelt among us, and *we have seen his glory*, glory as of the only Son from the Father, full of grace and truth. . . . For the law was given through Moses; grace and truth came through Jesus Christ.
>
> JOHN 1:1, 4-5, 14, 17, EMPHASIS ADDED

Although John begins his Gospel all the way back in the beginning, alluding to the Creation narrative in Genesis, he catapults us forward into Jesus' appearance on the scene with the verb *shine*. The entire passage turns on it. After using the past tense exclusively—"In the beginning *was*," the Word *was*," "In him *was*," "the life *was*"—John says the light *shines* (present tense) in the darkness. Right here, right now, the light shines. The light is continually shining; it cannot cease shining because "the very essence of light [is] that it shines."[4]

According to John, the shine took on human form. It dwelt, it tabernacled, it pitched its tent, it lived among us. John knew that the shining glory of God is formless, transcendent, unapproachable, but he had experienced divine shine as embodied, immanent, and approachable in the form of Jesus. He had *seen* the shine of the Son with his own eyes.

The word John uses that is translated *seen* or *beheld* "is invariably used in John (as, for that matter, in the whole New Testament) of seeing with the bodily eye. It is not used of visions. John is speaking of that glory which was seen in the literal, physical Jesus of Nazareth."[5] We have *seen* God's glory, explains John, and the light didn't blind us; it enabled us to see.

• • •

It's the middle of July, and the summer sky is blazing white. My son glances up at the sun, high and hot. He squints and asks, "Mom, is it true that if you look straight at the sun, you'll go blind?"

Science was never my subject. But experiencing a recent solar eclipse taught me that this little bit of folk wisdom is based on verifiable fact, not exaggerated fiction. I discourage him from testing it out himself, because right now the molten, fiery center of our solar system feels too close for comfort. The rays sear, and I find myself hustling toward the shade, ducking into shadow. I don't want to linger in the intensity of the shine.

Later, we walk to a nearby park for a picnic dinner. We settle down at a table tucked under a canopy of maple and plum branches. I look up and realize that I can truly appreciate the luminosity of the sun now, because the leaves filter the light in the most sublime way. The leaves aren't opaque like a brick wall or reflective like a glass mirror; they glow with diffused light, and they move in the breeze in a way that scatters the rays, shimmering over bark, stone walkways, and the strands of my kids' fair hair. The light passes *through* the leaves and is transformed into a bright, living veil, pierced with brilliance. The subtle beauty in this refracted light is lost when I step out of the shade directly into the overpowering radiance of the sun.

Jesus is a lot like those leaves. The glory shines *through* him in a way that makes the blinding brightness of divine holiness observable. And once seen, shine begins its work in us.

Shine That Enables Us to See

When I think of the dramatic shine of the Transfiguration, it seems hard to believe that it can illuminate my daily life. But I desperately need the shine this morning. So I pull back the opaque curtains in my bedroom to let in the morning light. Lying at the foot of the bed is a book on the iconography of the Transfiguration. The image on the cover is a reproduction of an eleventh-century fresco in the apse of Karanlık Kilise (the Dark Church) in Cappadocia, Turkey. The *mandorla* (glowing circle) of light surrounding Christ is perfectly circular. Its center is dark blue, and the radiance emanating from Jesus is represented by two outer rings that are progressively lighter in hue.

My two-year-old daughter is standing at the foot of the bed, her chin resting on the mattress right beside the book cover. I look into her eyes, still teary from a tantrum she just threw. Already this morning, she's stretched my patience thin to breaking. Up at five thirty in the morning demanding juice, then milk, then juice again, she was furious I didn't honor her request to have cookies for breakfast. Then we crossed ways again over her refusal to have her diaper changed. She raged through the entire process, no doubt waking the neighbors above and below. There is an irrationality particular to willful toddlers that leaves me so frustrated I feel myself teetering on the verge of violence.

And that's when I look up and see in her eyes the same sphere of radiant blue that encompasses Christ in the fresco—her dark inscrutable iris, ringed by smoky blue, surrounded by milky white. The light in her eyes perfectly mirrors the light of the Transfiguration on the reproduction on the book cover. I can't avoid the similarity of the shine. And I stagger inside. The light that struck the disciples on Tabor, humbling them to the ground, pierces me, too. This child who whittles my patience down to nothing has that same light in her eyes—if I can see past my frustration to that indelible image stamped into her being—*the image of God.*

Here I am still blurry from sleeplessness but immediately aware that I have to wake up to that image. The shine exposes the flint in my heart—my impatience, my self-centeredness—and it forces me to confront my sin and weakness and ask the Lord to change me. That's the power of the shine—it leaves me longing to be illuminated, more responsive, more radiant.

It occurs to me that it was the shine that arrested the apostle Paul on the road to Damascus, initiating a change so profound that a man hunting Christians with intent to kill was transformed into one of the pillars of the church. In Acts 22, when Paul describes the encounter with Jesus that completely reoriented his life, shine defined the moment:

"A great light from heaven suddenly *shone* around me. And I fell to the ground. . . . And since *I could not see because of the brightness of that light*, I was led by the hand by those who were with me" (Acts 22:6-7, 11, emphasis added).

The shock of the intensity of divine shine initially left Paul in darkness—blind, stumbling, and dependent—but over time, it enabled him to see with a clarity that completely altered his understanding of Jesus' identity. In his second letter to the Corinthian church, he explains, "For God, who said, 'Let light shine out of darkness,' has shone in our hearts to give the light of the knowledge of the glory of God in the face of Jesus Christ" (4:6). The light that initially blinded Paul lit up his interior world, emanating through his mind and soul.

My encounter with shine this morning may not be a radical, on-the-road-to-Damascus sort of moment, but the internal shift it's inspiring will make all the difference to the little one standing with her chin propped up on the edge of my mattress.

Receiving the Authority to Bless

In the Old Testament, there are two primary fountains of blessing—priests and family. A person received a blessing either from a priest who had been given authority to bless by God or from a family member, usually a father or elder brother. At Sinai, when God authored the blessing to be said over his people, he was particular about who was given authority to pronounce the blessing. God selected Aaron and his sons, the tribe of Levi, the tribe of priests.

As priests, Aaron and his sons were privileged in the nearness they enjoyed to God, but their privilege carried responsibility with it. They led Israel in worship *and* they mediated God's blessing to the people. The priestly job of blessing the people was an integral part of their service to the Lord, as Deuteronomy 21:5 makes clear: "The Levitical priests must step forward, for the LORD your God has chosen them to minister before him *and to pronounce blessings in the LORD's name*" (NLT, emphasis added). The responsibility to bless was a sacred trust given to a particular group for the sake of the whole nation.

The law given at Sinai delineated one tribe to serve as priests, and those men were obliged to submit to a complicated system of purification rites to approach the Holy Place suffused with God's presence. But Christ's ministry established a new covenant that obliterated the biological requirement for membership in the priesthood. Unlike the Levites, whose service to God was naturally limited by a human life span, Jesus "holds his priesthood permanently, because he continues forever" (Hebrews 7:24). According to Hebrews, Jesus is the supreme high priest, "holy, innocent, unstained, separated from sinners, and exalted above the heavens" (7:26), and as such, he offered the one sacrifice to end all sacrifices—himself.

When we draw near to Jesus as high priest, we, too, are welcomed into the priestly order. Peter tells us that as we come to Christ in faith, "you yourselves like living stones are being built up as a spiritual house, *to be a holy priesthood*, to offer spiritual sacrifices acceptable to God through Jesus Christ" (1 Peter 2:5, emphasis added). In Christ, the spiritual DNA necessary to bless is inscribed into our hearts. The rite of blessing once given to the Levites alone has been extended to us.

Within the old covenant, priests mediated God's blessing to the people, but as children of a new covenant, we're called to mediate God's goodness and grace to one another. Anyone in Christ can bless, because in Christ, we are both priests *and* family. The two primary contexts for blessing in the Old Testament become essential elements of the identity of a people called in Christ to carry God's blessing to a world still reeling from the curse.

"You are a chosen race," Peter elaborates, "*a royal priesthood, a holy nation, a people for his own possession, that you may proclaim the excellencies of him who called you out of darkness into his marvelous light*" (2:9, emphasis added). In this passage, Peter is not speaking to a group of seminary students. He's not addressing a church synod. He's not singling out those gifted as apostles, elders, or teachers. He's not tailoring his comments for the ordained. He is saying you—*plural*—all of you who believe in Christ are a royal priesthood and a holy nation, *a new Israel*, called to bear the light that now shines within you into the world. We are required to bless because "giving blessing . . . is now no longer, as in later layers of the Old Testament and Judaism, the special right of the priests, but is assigned *to all* as a charge."[6]

Tangible Shine: Spontaneous Expressions of Love

Initially, the charge to bless may seem daunting because of the formality associated with the priestly position. But blessings don't have to be formal to be powerful. The blessings that have touched me most deeply have been unexpected, spontaneous expressions of love that arrived when I most needed them, like the day during exam week at university when I found a bushel of fresh vegetables and half a homemade pound cake in a basket on the step of my college dorm room.

As soon as I saw the golden crust of the cake nestled beside the vine-ripe tomatoes, I knew they were gifts from Mary Jo, a woman who scattered shine in the most casual, unhurried way possible. Her house was a stone's throw from campus, so it was easy to wander there. Her front porch, her kitchen, her garden had become a refuge for me. In my mind's eye, I can still picture her bending over to clip fresh mint from a patch by her back step to brew tea. She always had something delicious on hand, but it wasn't the food I went for; I went for the shine.

When I was in Mary Jo's kitchen, I found that the stress of study lifted in the presence of light. Her generous, unvarnished hospitality and heartfelt prayers drew me back into the presence of God. Mary Jo was a priest to me: she mediated God's blessing by taking me back to Jesus' feet, reminding me of my spiritual home. On my wedding day, she gave a formal blessing as part of the ceremony; but the blessings that mattered most were all the cumulative, informal blessings lavished on me in the warm glow of the lamp hanging over her kitchen table.

I pull a thin, blue book with a dust jacket so worn that it is disintegrating off the bookshelf—*Gold by Moonlight* by Amy Carmichael. It was a gift from Mary Jo, along with the other books beside it, all editions of works by the woman known to her friends as *Amma,* a name that means "mother" in Tamil. Amy was founder of the Dohnavur Fellowship in India, a mission that, among other things, provided a home for young girls rescued from temple prostitution. Flipping through the pages yellowed by years, I realize that Amy's writing must have resonated with Mary Jo: They shared a conviction that blessing received must be poured out on others, that the light that runs through the pages of Scripture is for all the families of the earth, that God's shine is often most clearly perceived in practical acts of mercy. In so many ways, Amy's ministry embodied the prophetic vision of Isaiah, who perceived that "your light will break forth like the dawn" (Isaiah 58:8, NIV) when you lose the chains of injustice.

> If you do away with the yoke of oppression,
>   with the pointing finger and malicious talk,
> and if you spend yourselves in behalf of the
>   hungry
>   and satisfy the needs of the oppressed,
> *then your light will rise in the darkness,*
>   *and your night will become like the noonday.*
> ISAIAH 58:9-10, NIV, EMPHASIS ADDED

Amy, an Irishwoman from the village of Millisle not far from Belfast, never left India after her arrival in 1895. She spent her life on a coastland half a world away from the emerald island where she was born. Even after a devastating accident left her in intense physical pain for the last twenty years of her life, she continued to minister through writing. In a particularly incandescent passage in *Gold by Moonlight,*

she reflected on the urgency of living in the reality of the
shine anticipated in the priestly blessing:

> There are two notable effects of light in this part of
> Southern India. One is seen on a clear evening when
> the terra-cotta earth of the Plains, and every brick
> and tile made of that earth, takes on a brief and
> amazing brightness. The other is still more fugitive.
> It is never seen except in thundery weather, and then
> only on the hills that run down the western coast
> like a spine set out of place. The sun's rays striking
> up from the sea in sunrise are flung back by the
> thunder-cloud, and falling on mountain and forest
> turn the whole world to rose. The loveliness of such
> moments is unearthly. . . . All your soul worships.
>
> The beauty passes. The rose-light melts into the
> light of day, and in this it is a figure of the true.
> There are certain glories that are brief, like those
> lovely lights, but there is the common sunlight that
> is the life of every day. We live far too little in this
> light of life. . . . "Lord, lift Thou up the light of Thy
> countenance upon us." If we lived in the light of
> that Countenance, continually filled by the God of
> Hope with all joy and peace in believing, the dreary
> question, Who will show us any good? would be
> answered.[7]

When we bless one another with the words "May Yahweh
make His face shine on you," it has immediate application:
May God's face illuminate you today; may you walk in the

light of his presence right now; may you experience his bright shine in this culture tinged with gray; may you reflect the glory and goodness of God to those you meet. But the immediacy of the blessing never fully eclipses the ultimate future hope—the eschatological vision—of living in the wonder of eternal shine:

> The sun shall be no more
> your light by day,
> nor for brightness shall the moon
> give you light;
> but the LORD will be your everlasting light,
> and your God will be your glory.
>
> ISAIAH 60:19

Turning Leaving into Blessing

Just last week I had to say good-bye to a dear friend. Although this good-bye was one in a long string of good-byes, it felt sharper than most. The richness of our shared history had accumulated over a decade together living as foreigners in a city that can be in turns dazzling and mystifying. Laurel and I had watched one another's kids grow from toddlers to teenagers; we had swapped books, recipes, and parenting advice. She had brought meals at opportune times when I hadn't even requested them, showered me before the birth of a baby, and visited when my son was hospitalized, treating us to a batch of homemade oatmeal cookies. We had read Scripture together, prayed together, wondered together. She had counseled me, convicted me, and inspired me. She had been there for celebrations and on days when I felt like I was drowning. We had done life together. Friends scatter grace through the ins and outs of weeks. And this friend in particular had been full of those daily graces that infuse joy into the routine of daily living. How do you say good-bye to a friend like that?

Apparently, you say it over a good lunch and a good cup of coffee—or at least, that's how we decided to say it. We lingered long after we finished eating, as if we were reluctant to part with the white mugs that looked so pristine on the white tile table. A part of me wanted to stay right there. But life moves forward, and at some point, we have to rise and move with it.

So we stood and embraced. I wanted her to know that there was nothing I wanted more than for her to go with the shine, with the grace, with the favor, with the peace. In sum, I wanted her to go surrounded by the presence of God. Holding her, I whispered through tears, "May God bless you, may he keep you, may his face shine on you . . ."

Whenever I pray these words, a flood of images races through my mind. I am thinking of Sinai and Mount Tabor, of Moses' radiant skin and of Jesus' brilliant, transfigured form. I am remembering the shine on the road to Damascus and anticipating the fulfillment of Isaiah's marvelous vision of eternal shine and the arrival of a city that has "no need of sun or moon to shine on it, for *the glory of God gives it light, and its lamp is the Lamb*" (Revelation 21:23, emphasis added). As my mind scrolls through all the allusions packed into such a concise blessing, I wonder if the words might break under the strain. But these words aren't fragile; they're elastic and expansive and eternal. The words of the blessing aren't weighed down by the associations; they are enlivened by them.

I barely got through the blessing. My voice faltered and cracked, but I stumbled through every wonderful word and then added a few of my own. I wanted to speak the blessing in its entirety.

I was so focused on the blessing, in fact, that I had forgotten to pay the bill. It's always irritating when logistical necessity intrudes on an emotional moment, but while wiping tears from my cheek and blotting at my smeared mascara, I pushed my chair away from the table and got our waiter's attention. We stepped out of the restaurant together, but on the sidewalk, we parted ways. I walked on, knowing she was going with the shine and that when we meet again, the shine will be there with us.

Fill me afresh with hope, O God of hope,
That undefeated I may climb the hill
As seeing Him who is invisible,
Whom having not seen I love.
O my Redeemer, when this little while
Lies far behind me and the last defile
Is all alight, and in that light I see
My Saviour and my Lord, what will it be?

AMY CARMICHAEL, *GOLD BY MOONLIGHT*, 1935

chapter 5

INSPIRATION
FOR BLESSING

BEYOND MAGIC

*May our hearts not yield
to the words of the wicked;
deliver us from all
who seek to take possession of our souls.
For our eyes are fixed on you, O Lord,
our refuge is in you and you are our hope.*

A GREEK ORTHODOX BLESSING FOR VESPERS,
THE BARBERINI CODEX 336, EIGHTH CENTURY,
PRAYING WITH THE ORTHODOX TRADITION

"Sleeping Beauty" is one of those stories that glows with the patina of age—a tale so old that it is nearly impossible to pinpoint its origin. From the beginning of the story, we find ourselves in a world where good is at odds with evil, where blessing and curse are taken seriously, where the spoken word conjures up future reality.

We all know the contours of the story. At a party celebrating the birth of a princess, the plot is set into motion when a series of blessings are interrupted by one powerful curse: The princess will prick her finger on a spinning needle and die. A final blessing softens the blow somewhat by transforming death into a deep sleep. The telling of this story with the strongest foothold in my memory is the Disney film that was popular when I was a child. In that imaginative version, the blessings were given by spritely fairies wearing Technicolor dresses gleefully, although perhaps overzealously, wielding their magic wands. But before there was Disney, there were the Brothers Grimm.

I leave a cup of green tea steeping on the table beside my bed and sneak into my daughter's room. She's sound asleep, so I search for the book I'm looking for in the dark. Just below her collection of Nancy Drew mysteries, I find a leather-bound edition of *Grimm's Complete Fairy Tales*. The gold scrollwork on the cover framing a painting of a forlorn-looking Rapunzel wrapped in her serpentine hair was designed to look old and venerable, but the edition is, in fact, brand-new. Retreating back to my room, I scan the titles of the stories in the table of contents. Somewhere between "The Devil's Sooty Brother" and "Fair Katrinelje and Pif-Paf-Poltrie," I find "Sleeping Beauty."

In Grimm's version, it's not flighty fairies who deliver blessings to the new baby, it is *wise women*—flesh-and-blood women who are attributed the ability to bless and to curse. At the end of the feast celebrating the arrival of the princess, "*the Wise women* bestowed their magic gifts upon the baby." Twelve wise women bless, but one vindictive, malicious woman curses. Her corrosive words are fashioned to steal joy and strangle life.

If there's one thing the story gets right, it's that the essence of curse is the will to destroy. In the tale "Sleeping Beauty," the cruel curse seeks to devastate a mother and father by stealing the life of their child.

"Sleeping Beauty" might have been published in the seventeenth century, but it reflects a much older oral tradition of storytelling that taps into the pagan practice of blessing and cursing. In the ancient world, and in many places where folk religion is practiced today, blessing and cursing fall in the realm of magic. This traditional understanding of the practice was deeply rooted in the cultures of the Amorites, Moabites, Canaanites, and Amalekites, who lived in and around the land that God promised to Israel. They believed their region was full of spirits and local gods who occupied holy places, especially high places. Mediums, seers, and pagan priests seemed to have special access to these gods. They could divine the future, look for omens, communicate with the dead, and speak words that many believed were imbued with special power to bless or to curse. In Numbers 22–24, we meet one of these men, Balaam the son of Beor, a Mesopotamian prophet whose blessing or curse could be bought for a price.

The Opposite of Cursing

Let me provide a little context for Balaam's story: After being freed by God from slavery in Egypt, the Israelites had wandered in the desert for forty years. But finally, they were approaching the border of the Promised Land. They had defeated the Amorites, occupied their cities, and were camping out on the plains of Moab near the old city of Jericho.

Meanwhile, the Moabites had been watching the Israelite advance with dread. Balak, the king of Moab, knew he was backed into a corner. So he sent a delegation of princes to Balaam, hoping to buy a powerful curse that would turn the tide against Israel. Along with money, the king sent Balaam a message brimming with confidence in his abilities: "Come now, curse this people for me . . . for I know that he whom you bless is blessed, and he whom you curse is cursed" (Numbers 22:6).

The stage is set for a showdown. Is the king's confidence in Balaam justified? Can the power of a local pagan seer to curse overcome God's promise to bless Israel? Are the local gods as powerful as the God of Abraham, Isaac, and Jacob? With whom does the ultimate authority to bless and curse really rest?

Not many of us would hire a professional like Balaam to curse our enemies, but we may be tempted to curse in more subtle ways. When we feel offended or wounded, when someone is invading our space, or worse, threatening one of our kids, a family member, or a friend, we might not speak a curse aloud but our thoughts can devolve into a silent vehicle for cursing. Dallas Willard explains that "a curse is the projection of evil on someone. It's using language or attitudes that project evil into their lives."[1] When we curse, we use language *or* attitudes. Cursing may be verbal *or* nonverbal, but in either case, it bites. Interacting with others with an attitude that communicates cursing can be just as devastating to healthy relationships as a curse expressed in words.

A curse is an offensive gesture from a defensive position. When we've been hurt or feel threatened, our frustration and fear often coalesce around anger until we find ourselves dwelling on, even wishing for, the destruction or demotion of the one who hurt us. Curses shoot out of our mouths like poisoned darts—they're words meant to inflict pain. They sting the moment they hit their mark, and the resulting wound festers in the future as the words work their way under the skin of the heart. The pins and needles stuck in voodoo dolls are just a physical representation of what curses are meant to do at the psychic and emotional level.

Blessing and cursing are polar opposites. Blessing flows out of generosity of spirit that desires good for another, while cursing is inspired by evil intent. Blessing builds up; cursing tears down. Blessing invites others to draw near; cursing pushes them away. Blessing invokes peace; cursing inflicts division. Blessing frees another to new possibilities; cursing seeks to shackle the future. Blessing is proactive; cursing is reactive.

Cursing is like offering someone a cup of poisoned water from a polluted well. James says that if we use our tongues to bless God, we can't turn around and in the next breath curse a person made in God's image. We can't sing praises on Sunday and then belittle our coworkers on Monday. "No one can tame the tongue;" observes James, "it is a restless evil and full of deadly poison. With it we bless our Lord and Father, and with it we curse men, who have been made in the likeness of God; from the same mouth come both blessing and cursing. My brethren, *these things ought not to be this way.* Does a fountain send out from the same opening both fresh and bitter water?" (James 3:8-11, NASB, emphasis added).

God never allows his people to curse; he encourages them to *lament.* God doesn't expect us to bottle up our hurt and our fear, suppressing it unnaturally; he encourages us to turn toward him and pour out our hearts. This is what we see David, the shepherd anointed king of Israel, doing again and again in the Psalms.[2]

How long, LORD? Will you forget me forever?
How long will you hide your face from me?
How long must I wrestle with my thoughts
and day after day have sorrow in my heart?
How long will my enemy triumph over me?

PSALM 13:1-2, NIV

This is the groaning of lament. Lamentation is a way to express our frustration, our discouragement, our terror, and our desire for justice to God, laying all our angst and confusion at his feet, begging him to judge justly and right the wrongs that cause suffering. Lamentation trusts that God hears, sees, is in control, and will respond in his own time. Cursing, on the other hand, is attempting to take matters into our own hands, exercising verbal judgment by damning or defaming another. Cursing gives voice to fear, while lamentation is an expression of faith. God invites us to reflect his character by blessing, but he doesn't extend the authority to judge by allowing us to curse.

Shielded from Curse

"What have you got in here?" I ask my son, slinging his backpack over my shoulder. "Did you fill your bag with rocks?"

He's complaining the bag is too heavy to carry, so I lug it up the hill home.

Dropping the bag inside the front door, I unzip it and pull out a stone the size of my palm. It's painted dark blue with the image of a bright blue eye in the middle. It's a *nazar boncuk*, a charm to protect from the curse of the evil eye.

Nazar boncuk are everywhere in Turkey. I see them emblazoned on the backs of minibuses, painted on ceramics, hanging over doorways, woven into entry rugs, spun into glass, and incorporated into beaded jewelry. I've had kind, concerned women pin them on my kids at the bazaar. A dear friend hand-knit a gorgeous peacock-blue sweater for my son—every button was a nazar boncuk. I've always appreciated the sentiment behind these gifts. They communicate care. People who give nazar boncuk want our family to be protected; they want us to be safe from harm. Nazar boncuk are given with love. But behind them is fear—fear of malevolent spirits, fear of disaster, fear of curse.

Because I grew up in a Western, secularized culture, I didn't grow up with an instinctive fear of curse. From the vantage point of a post-Enlightenment worldview that tends to dismiss supernatural forces out of hand, curses are woven into the fabric of fairy tales like "Sleeping Beauty," not into real life. Extreme skepticism regarding supernatural forces may characterize the outlook of modern society, but it's not consistent with the biblical worldview. The Bible doesn't deny the presence of malignant spiritual influences like the serpent whispering in the Garden, evil spirits, or pagan gods. The people of Israel were often tempted to tap into these dark powers. King Saul's visit to the witch of Endor, Ahab's reliance on the priests of Baal, or Manasseh's practice of witchcraft and divination all testify to the destructive appeal of spiritual practices God explicitly prohibited.[3] But whenever God confronted these forces, he either overpowered them or judged them. And that's precisely what happened during God's encounter with Balak the king and his prophet Balaam.

Between Balaam's reluctant acceptance of his task to curse Israel and his arrival in Moab, the story veers off in an unexpectedly comic direction. The prophet sets off riding his faithful donkey, but along the way, she charges off the path into a field. Furious, Balaam strikes her, forcing her back onto the road. Again, she balks, crushing his foot against a rock wall, and again, he punishes her. Still refusing to move forward, she lies down. Balaam vents his rage by beating her yet again, his cruelty a glimpse into his true character. All along we know (because the narrator tells us) that the donkey sees the angel of the LORD standing in the road with a sword raised. The donkey's defiance is an act of mercy—she's attempting to save Balaam's life.

At this pivotal moment, God gives the donkey a voice of her own. The animal speaks, chiding Balaam for beating her and reminding him of her trustworthy service over the years. Startled out of his anger, the seer finally sees.

We cannot miss the irony that Balaam, *the seer*, the one who was paid for his spiritual insight and power, had less spiritual discernment than a donkey. This vignette works to foreshadow events about to unfold: Three times, Balaam, like his donkey, will find himself uncomfortably caught between the will of a pagan man and the word of God. Three times, Balaam will be commanded to curse; and three times, God will direct him to bless. The parallelism "suggests that the ability to declare God's word is not necessarily a sign of Balaam's holiness, only that God can use anyone to be his spokesman."[4]

So let's get this straight: Balaam is not a man of God. In this passage, it might appear that Balaam has a good rapport with God because he speaks the blessings the Lord's Spirit inspires, but he later leads Israel into idolatry.[5] Balaam, in his own power, never could have conjured up these illuminating words with a prophetic edge. In this situation, the Spirit *momentarily* fills an imperfect man in order to say what needs to be said.

Our discussion of Isaac and Jacob in chapter 3 demonstrated that blessing begins with seeing. And in the last chapter, we saw that in Christ, we've been given the authority to bless. Balaam's story suggests that the source of the spiritual vision and inspiration to bless comes from the indwelling of God's Spirit. Numbers 24:2 says that the Spirit of God *came upon* Balaam. In the Old Testament, the Spirit of God was given only to a few and only temporarily, to fulfill a particular purpose. But the prophet Joel envisioned a day when God's Spirit would be poured out on all his sons and daughters (Joel 2:28-29). Jesus promised that he would send the Spirit to live in us—to comfort, convict, counsel, and guide us to truth (John 14:15-17, 25-26; 16:12-13). On the day of Pentecost, the promise was realized when Jesus' disciples "were all filled with the Holy Spirit" (Acts 2:4). In Christ, the same Spirit fills us, giving us life, transforming us into the image of the Lord, impressing the Word of God on our hearts (2 Corinthians 1:21-22; 3:3-18). When it comes to communicating blessing, we depend on the Spirit to give us discernment to be able to speak truth that is suited to a person in a particular moment.

God spoke through Balaam not because Balaam was a man of God, but because God was proving that his Spirit was more powerful than the spirits Balaam was accustomed to serving. In the Bible, there's no physical object or incantation that protects from the threat of curse; instead, there's a living God who shelters those who turn to him for refuge. No curse can touch the people God has blessed.

Balaam was well aware that his power paled in comparison to God's power, a point he was anxious to convey to the king as soon as the two met: "How can I curse those whom God has not cursed? How can I denounce those whom the LORD has not denounced?" (Numbers 23:8, NIV). These rhetorical questions are the prelude to a univocal blessing,

> He considers no disaster for Jacob;
> He sees no trouble for Israel.
> The LORD their God is with them,
> and there is rejoicing over the King among them.

> God brought them out of Egypt;
> He is like the horns of a wild ox for them.
> There is no magic curse against Jacob
> and no divination against Israel.
>
> NUMBERS 23:21-23, HCSB

Each of Balaam's messages allude to God's covenant blessing of Abraham, Isaac, and Jacob. But in addition to affirming the trustworthiness of God, Balaam's prophecy reveals future hope, shining a light on what will come. Balaam envisions the nation of Israel flourishing in the land "like gardens beside a river. . . . Water will flow from their buckets; their seed will have abundant water" (Numbers 24:6-7, NIV). Water does not normally *flow* from buckets; it sits stagnant in them. But life-giving water is going to flow through Israel. There is going to be an inexhaustible, uncontainable river of living water that will sustain the people of God and flow out to others. This blessing evokes the state of blessing we first observed in Eden and anticipates a return to an existence defined by blessing. God's blessing illuminates the future. His words shine a light on what will come. Whereas "we use the word *foreshadow* for the imperfect representation of something that is yet to come," John O'Donahue writes, "we could say that a blessing 'forebrightens' the way."[6]

Christian blessing is not magic—it's intervention and intercession. When God blesses, he intervenes in our lives, communicating truth, sustaining us with good, saving us from harm. When we bless one another, we're interceding. We may ask God to act, save, provide, counsel, comfort, shepherd, and redeem—all blessings consistent with truth revealed in Scripture. Christian blessing is a particular kind of intercession that prays forward clinging to the promises of God with the faith that he will accomplish them in the lives of those for whom we pray. The inspiration for blessing comes from two primary sources: God's Word and the indwelling of God's Spirit.

When Curse Is Turned into Blessing

It would be easy to stop right here—to dwell on the good of the blessing without mentioning God's judgment on Moab. But that would be to gloss over the aspects of this story that may be troubling. After blessing Israel, Balaam prophesies that God will annihilate his adversaries, breaking their bones in pieces and piercing them with his arrows—harsh words in the context of a blessing (Numbers 24:8). In passages like this, I'm reminded of the chasm of cultural distance that separates me from those who populate the stories in Scripture. I haven't lived in a world scarred by tribal warfare and pagan rituals, but that is the landscape I'm occupying when I dive into the Old Testament. A succeeding king of Moab will later offer his oldest son as a human sacrifice to the god Chemosh to save his own skin (2 Kings 3:27).[7] It is this savage brand of idolatry that God intends to guard against by judging Moab and other pagan nations.

I pause to remember how this chapter fits into the bigger story of God's relationship with humanity. The God revealed in the Old Testament is not cruel; he is merciful, gracious, patient, abounding in love and faithfulness (Exodus 34:6). And he chose Israel, a particular nation, so that Israel would be a blessing to *all the nations of the earth*—including adversaries like Moab. We begin to glimpse the healing of the fractured relationship between Moab and Israel in the story of an Israeli widow named Naomi and her Moabite daughter-in-law, Ruth. The book of Ruth, set in a time after Balaam's prophesy had been delivered, beautifully illustrates what Israel's relationship with neighboring peoples can look like when it is defined by mutual blessing.

The bare bones of the story go like this: Naomi's family moves to Moab, and both Naomi's sons marry Moabite women. When the men die, Naomi frees her Moabite daughters-in-law to remarry, but Ruth clings to Naomi and returns with her to Israel, saying, "Your people shall be my people, and your God, my God" (Ruth 1:16, NASB). Naomi advises Ruth, helping her find a worthy husband named Boaz, with whom she has a child.

The tender love and respect that mark Ruth and Naomi's relationship from beginning to end demonstrates that a woman from Moab can be welcomed into Israel's family not as a peripheral, marginalized foreigner, but as an honored member *blessed* by the entire community. Repeatedly in the telling of the story, we're reminded that Ruth is a Moabite— her nationality is almost always associated with her name.[8] But Ruth is not devoted to the Moabite god Chemosh; she commits herself to Naomi and to Naomi's God. She blesses Naomi with loyalty, and consequently she's blessed by everyone she encounters—first by Naomi, twice by Boaz, and finally by the entire community.[9] "All the people who were at the gate and the elders" pronounce a blessing over the couple: "May the LORD make the woman, who is coming into your house, like Rachel and Leah, who together built up the house of Israel" (4:11). We soon see the blessing realized when Ruth bears a son named Obed, who becomes the father of Jesse, who becomes the father of King David, Israel's greatest king (Ruth 4:17).

Reading Balaam's prophecy anticipating the defeat of Moab alongside the story of the Moabite Ruth, we realize that God's protection of Israel and judgment of Moab serve a greater purpose—*Moab's redemption*. God protects Israel from Balak's attempt to curse, turning the curse into a blessing, *because* Israel has been chosen to be a blessing to, among others, Moab! The fact that a Moabite woman becomes the great-grandmother of the future king of Israel demonstrates that through God's blessing, seemingly irreconcilable differences between warring peoples can be healed. Enemies can become friends. Enemies can even become family.

Fragile Threads of Blessing

Light rain falls and glosses the upper deck of the boat. I'm sitting on a bench under an awning that's keeping most of the cold precipitation off my head. I wish my coat had a hood. As we move away from the dock, I wrap my scarf tighter around my neck, bracing against the chill of the morning breeze off the Marmara Sea. It's April, but it's early and overcast. Later, when the sun breaks through the carpet of clouds, it'll be hot, and I'll regret I wore a sweater.

I'm on my way to an island not far from Istanbul. Twice a year, women desperate for a blessing make a pilgrimage to Hagios Georgios Koudounas—or Saint George of the

Bells—a church and monastery that crown the highest hill. There's been a church on the summit for at least a thousand years. It's said that a shepherd whose sheep were grazing in the vicinity heard bells ringing below the ground. When the villagers dug to find the source of the melody, they discovered an icon of Saint George. After the icon was enshrined in a church on the spot where it was unearthed, legend surrounding the image grew. It was rumored that it could heal disease, free people from demonic spirits, and grant blessings.[10]

I hike up past the elegant summer homes lining the avenues at the base of the island on the way to a square ringed with horses and carriages. It's here that the footpath leading up to the monastery begins. I pass a woman with her feet bare, her toes gripping the stone, her head bowed in prayer. Only the most devout pilgrims walk the path barefoot. Everyone else is in sneakers or sandals.

For the most part, the atmosphere feels like an open-air carnival. Vendors line the walk up the hill selling cooking oil to give as an offering to the monks who tend the monastery. There are seasonal fruits, handstitched bags, jewelry, trinkets, ringlets of flowers to wear in your hair. Many of the tables display tiny colored ribbons, each with a different tag—red for love, pink for a baby, green for prosperity, orange for a job, and white for healing. Each ribbon is a blessing for sale.

Spools of colored thread are lined up alongside the ribbons. Women buy a spool representing the blessing they most long for, then carefully unwind the string as they walk ever upward, leaving their longing trailing behind them, fragile and tenuous. It's rumored that if you manage to arrive at the top with your string unbroken, then your wish—*your blessing*—is guaranteed to be granted.

Balak paid Balaam to curse his enemies, which is a roundabout way of purchasing the blessing of protection. And it occurs to me that our fears are often the flip side of our longings. The longing for love—the yearning for a husband or wife—is often intimately related to the fear of being left alone. The longing for healing may be the alternate side of the fear of suffering unrelenting pain. The longing for success at work or school is often intertwined with fear of failure. My greatest fear—the loss of one of my children to terminal illness, a traumatic accident, or violence—is surely related to my longing for God to protect them. Our longings for blessings are intricately intertwined with our fears like mottled thread spun in the depths of our being.

The idea that God's favor and protection can be bought knits together an old story and an ancient approach to divinity with a practice still very much alive today. Many people still deal with God as if his attention can be earned, as if a blessing can be "called down by an appropriately formulated prayer" and a particular kind of offering. But as D. A. Carson notes, "that sort of view is almost akin to pagan magic; it is only a whisker from raw animism."[11] Churches are transformed into pagan temples when we begin to think God's blessing comes with a price tag. "The bestowal of blessing was once a magical rite," observes Old Testament scholar Claus Westermann, "but this magical quality was first eliminated in the Old Testament not in the New. It occurred through the way in which God's promise was combined with the history of God's people."[12]

As I walk up the path, I find myself treading lightly, trying not to break a string. My caution isn't a sign of my belief in the power of this tradition; it reflects my empathy for these women unspooling their souls. Surveying the tangle of delicate strings threaded through the bushes all along the path, I imagine so many hearts unwound, strung out, stretched taut. My steps slow, not because the path is too steep but because my heart is heavy. Blessings were never meant to be traded, bartered, bought. God's blessing is never—*never ever*—for sale. If you could buy blessing, then it would be a transaction, not a gift. And blessing is a gift, *always* a gift. No strings attached.

There's no price we could pay that would purchase forgiveness, no check we could write that would buy us the presence of God throughout our days, no credit card that can guarantee entrance into eternal life in the new heavens and new earth, where there are no tears, no death, no curse. I have the impulse to grab these women unspooling their thread and cry that the peace they truly long for is freely offered, already given. If only they could grasp hold of the foundational truth that God has already "blessed us in Christ with *every* spiritual blessing in the heavenly places" (Ephesians 1:3, emphasis added).

But it's not like me to create a scene. So I pause to rest on a chair by the path. A beautiful woman with long raven hair sits down beside me. Her eye makeup is perfect, but her expression is pained. I greet her simply and ask her name, but she gestures that she's taken a vow of silence. She might have committed not to speak, but it seems to me she would like to. I tell her that I understand. You'd think that would have ended the one-sided conversation, but I find myself still glancing in her direction. I should probably get up and leave her to silent devotion, but I'm unable to move on. There's a catch in my spirit, an impulse to communicate some of the good that I believe God desires for her. She might be quiet, but she doesn't look like she's at peace.

I ask if I can pray for her, and she nods yes enthusiastically. I wonder what precisely I should say. I can't ask her about her deep wound or her deep desire. I don't know the nature of the longing that prompted her to come to this high mountain. I don't have history with her to draw on in the way I did when composing a blessing for my daughter.

In situations like these, Scripture is an invaluable resource—alongside the counsel of the Holy Spirit, it's the primary inspiration for blessing. Paul's prayers, in particular, have a depth of meaning and theological precision that speak powerfully in moments of desperation and need. I could, for instance, pray hope for her: "May the God of hope fill you with all joy and peace in believing, so that by the power of the Holy Spirit you may abound in hope" (Romans 15:13). Or I could focus on knowledge of God's will and spiritual insight (Colossians 1:9-10) or bless her with comfort (2 Thessalonians 2:16-17) or peace (1 Thessalonians 5:23).

But it's not these blessings that come to mind. I look in her eyes and reach out to hold her hand. One of my favorite prayers from Paul's letter to the Ephesians informs my blessing for her. Not every phrase comes out perfectly. I improvise a little, filling in the pauses. But it seems right, because these words speak to a soul longing to be filled.

May you be strengthened with power through God's
    Spirit in your inner being,
  so that Christ may dwell in your hearts through
    faith;
And may you, being rooted and grounded in love,
be able to comprehend with all the saints
    the breadth and length and height and depth of the
      love of God
    and to know the love of Christ which surpasses
      knowledge,
that you may be filled up to all the fullness of God.

EPHESIANS 3:16-19, AUTHOR'S PARAPHRASE

chapter 6

SUSTAINING BLESSING

WHEN LIFE IS HARD

When evil darkens our world, give us light.
When despair numbs our souls, give us hope.

When we stumble and fall, lift us up.
When doubts assail us, give us faith.

JOHN D. RAYNER (1924–2005)

"*Blessed are you among women*, and blessed is the child in your womb," Elizabeth ecstatically exclaimed to Mary when the young girl turned up on her doorstep unexpected, pregnant, and not yet married. The last few days I've been thinking of this effusive greeting recorded in Luke 1:42 (NET). I've been turning it over in my mind while sitting in the sterile confines of a hospital room, observing the slow drip of IV fluids into my son's arm. And I've been wondering how it's possible to think of Mary as *most blessed*.

Mary doesn't exactly fit the public profile of a woman whom we'd consider blessed today. She wasn't rich. She didn't live in a chic home with midcentury furniture, granite countertops, and Sub-Zero kitchen appliances. She didn't have a comfortable margin in her 401(k) or send her kids to exclusive universities. She didn't have an enviable career. She wasn't safe, privileged, or fashionable. She would have been unlikely to have the word *blessed* embroidered on decorative pillows in her home. So in what sense was she *most blessed*?

In reality, she was poor. She and her family were villagers living in the oppressive shadow of an empire that saw them as a revenue stream. They were a people to tax, not to welcome as citizens. She never had the freedom to vote, the opportunity to study, the leisure time to relax by the Mediterranean Sea. There were no summer vacations for Mary. Not long after she delivered her first son, she fled with her husband to Egypt, living as a refugee in a foreign land in a desperate attempt to shield her son from the unhinged king seeking to end his life.

Luke 2:19 tells us that Mary was a ponderer. She treasured the moments surrounding Jesus' birth, holding them in her heart. When the poet W. H. Auden imagined the thoughts running through Mary's mind while she gazed on her new-born son's face, he supposed that she was already aware of the grief that would accompany the blessing:

Why was I chosen to teach His Son to weep?
   Little One, sleep.
Dream. In human dreams earth ascends to Heaven
Where no one need pray nor ever feel alone.
In your first few hours of life here, O have you
Chosen already what death must be your own?
How soon will you start on the Sorrowful Way?
Dream while you may.

W. H. AUDEN, *FOR THE TIME BEING*

I shudder for any mother who has to contemplate so soon the death of her son. What mother would feel blessed to live in the shadow of "the Sorrowful Way"?

My son stirs in the hospital bed. The surgical tape that keeps the IV secure in his vein itches his skin. I watch a little blood creeping up the line. I buzz the nurse to check it. She switches the bag, presses a button, and the slow, steady fluid drip resumes. Antibiotics flow into his little five-year-old body in the most immediate way possible.

He was hospitalized for bacterial pneumonia four days ago. My kids have always been susceptible to croup. They get it every winter we're in the city. He seemed to recover from a nasty virus. Since he'd been fever free for two days, I sent him back to school. But while we were walking home together, he started to wheeze. He complained that his throat hurt, but what he really meant was that air wouldn't fill his lungs.

I took him to see our pediatrician, thinking he might need an antibiotic. But as she listened to his lungs, the stethoscope pressed to his thin, heaving chest, I could see concern etched in her eyes. She sent us straight to the emergency room.

My son's face convulsed in panic the moment the nurse wheeled in the cart holding the syringe. I had to hold him down, gripping him like a vice so she could sink one needle into his thigh and then another into his wrist. He relaxed in my arms afterward, his tears evaporating to salty streaks on his cheeks. He stayed curled up in my lap, his arms cradling his knees to his chest as the nurse flipped the switch turning on the breathing treatment. The cool, moist air—a healing fog infused with medicine—filled the plastic mask covering his mouth and nose.

That was four interminably long days ago. Now it's Good Friday, two days before Easter. Between the frequent nurse visits to gather vital statistics and the delivery of plastic trays laden with bland food that he barely even touches, I've had plenty of time to think of all the "what-ifs": *What if he takes a turn for the worse? What if he has a reaction to the medication? What if his lung collapses? What if I lose him?*

Rationally, I know none of these what-ifs are likely to be realized, because we're receiving the best care available. But a mother's thoughts are not always rational when the life of a child is in the balance. When we're reminded that our kids' lives are fragile, a fierce, inexpressible force of emotion takes over. We feel a craving to spare them, to save them, to shield them from suffering. We long to take their pain ourselves.

The realization that we are unable to do so is the most awful realization of all.

During this hospital vigil that happens to coincide with Passion Week, I'm trying to redirect all my anxious thoughts. So I've been thinking about Mary. I'm hoping to learn how she endured watching her son suffer. I'm wondering how she lived through the grief of witnessing the Crucifixion. I'm longing to understand her embrace of blessing in suffering and loss.

The Impossible Blessing

When the angel Gabriel first visited Mary to tell her she had been chosen to carry the Son of the Most High, she understandably wondered, "How can this be?"

The angel explained, "The Holy Spirit will come upon you, and the power of the Most High will overshadow you." And then he comforted the anxious young woman with the reassuring promise: "For nothing will be impossible with God" (Luke 1:35-37, NASB).

It wasn't the first time Mary had heard the words *nothing will be impossible with God*. A young Jewish woman schooled in the stories of Abram and Sarai—later renamed Abraham and Sarah—would have known these words well because they featured prominently in the story of the birth of Isaac, the miracle child. The statement ties together the stories of two women separated by centuries who were both blessed by God to be carriers of the blessing that would flow to all the families of the earth. Like Mary, Sarah received the stunning news that she would become the mother of a son. Sarah's problem, however, was nothing like Mary's. Sarah wasn't a virgin; she was barren. She wasn't too young and innocent to carry a child; she was too old and exhausted.

At the very beginning of Abram and Sarai's story, we're told that Sarai "was barren; she had no child" (Genesis 11:30). Before we know anything else about her, we know she's unable to conceive—her identity was defined by her barrenness. Her infertility would have been a source of disappointment and shame before God's call and blessing of Abram, but after the blessing was spoken, it became the central crisis of the couple's story. How will a man with a barren wife become the father of a great nation? Given that fertility was an aspect of God's primal blessing, why would God choose this particular woman to bear a blessing meant for all families of the earth? Is God able to resurrect a barren womb?

Any woman who has struggled with infertility knows the heartache that accompanies the arrival of each monthly cycle. All the hurt accumulated over decades of waiting was bound to scar Sarah's soul. In her impatience and frustration, she blamed the Lord for her barrenness (Genesis 16:2). Then she took matters into her own hands. If God could not produce the promised child, then she would produce one for him. In an attempt to accomplish God's purpose in her own way, she encouraged her husband to sleep with her Egyptian servant, Hagar, who bore a son named Ishmael. But Sarah underestimated how bitterly she would be disappointed by this solution—*her own solution*—because, in the end, Hagar's fertility only emphasized her own emptiness.

After nearly a quarter century of waiting for the child

promised by God, the Lord visited Abraham and Sarah to tell them that the fulfillment of the blessing was imminent—that Sarah would have a son within the year. But by this time, Sarah was not only barren; she was ninety years old and post-menopausal. All of this intimate detail serves to demonstrate that there is no natural way the blessing can come to life (Genesis 17:15-19; 18:9-15). Any objective observer realizes that Sarah had good reason to doubt God's promise to bless her with a son.

But Sarah was not an objective observer. Her doubt and desire for rejuvenation collided in the depths of her being. Sarah felt the impossibility of blessing in the most intimate, tender place of her body and her soul. And so, in response to the prophetic word that she would bear a son, rather than weep for joy, she laughed.

Her laughter hinted at her disillusionment. Living in the wrenching space between the promise and its fulfillment, she must have felt torn between the desire to believe and the painful erosion of hope. Sarah wondered aloud, "After I am worn out, and my lord is old, shall I have pleasure?" (Genesis 18:12). I imagine Sarah reaching up to tuck a stray gray hair under her head scarf, her wrinkled hand alighting on her cheek once flush with youth, but now weathered by age, travel, and disappointment. She suspected that some things might be too hard for God.

Reflecting on the source of Sarah's laughter, Frederick Buechner suggests that "it comes from as deep a place as tears come from, and in a way it comes from the same place. As much as tears do, it comes out of the darkness of the world where God is of all missing persons the most missed, except that it comes not as an ally of darkness but as its adversary, not as a symptom of darkness but as its antidote."[1] If Buechner's insight that laughter is an antidote to darkness is on the mark, then Sarah's laughter is a sign that faith is winning the day in her internal battle with the darkness of doubt.

However thin Sarah's faith had been stretched, it didn't break. Posterity remembers Sarah not as a woman of doubt but as a woman of faith. The book of Hebrews links Sarah's faith to the healing of her barrenness: "By faith even Sarah herself received ability to conceive, even beyond the proper time of life, since she considered Him faithful who had promised" (11:11, NASB). In the end, Sarah's age and barrenness challenge our credulity. Do *we believe* God's blessing can reverse the effects of age on a woman's body? Can the one who designed the intricate mechanics of biological processes intervene supernaturally to upend the cycle? Can a barren woman birth a blessing?

Precisely at the point we may be tempted to doubt, the Lord responds with a restorative rebuke, "Is anything too hard for the LORD?" (Genesis 18:14).

If we answer yes to the Lord's question, saying that some things *are* too difficult for God, then "we have determined to live in a closed universe where things are stable, reliable, and hopeless."[2] This is precisely the sort of world that many people live in—a mechanistic world where nothing exists beyond what they can see, touch, and prove, where there is no need of faith because there can be no miracles, no divine interventions, no hope of rescue or blessing.

But as Mary contemplated the angel's declaration,

"Nothing is impossible with God," her faith overcame the mechanistic lie. She knew the end of Sarah's story—that God freed her from barrenness by blessing her with Isaac (Genesis 21:1-7). And then, Sarah laughed; but this time her laughter was unrestrained, joyous, celebratory, and contagious. This was laughter that welcomed others to the party. "God has made laughter for me," Sarah sang, "everyone who hears will laugh over me" (Genesis 21:6). The name *Isaac* means "he laughs."[3] First Sarah and Abraham laughed at the impossibility of the blessing. Then they laughed because the impossible came to life. And God laughed with them, memorializing their laughter in the name of their son, who forever would remind them of the joy that comes at the end of a long season of painful waiting.

I may be a lot like Sarah in her tendency to doubt, but I'd like to be more like Mary in her unwavering faith. Mary had learned from Sarah's experience, internalizing the narrative so that it shaped her perception of the possible. When the angel visited Mary to tell her she would be blessed with a son in spite of her virginity, she didn't laugh; she believed.

Blessed Are Those Who Mourn

We can't know for sure if Mary was already thinking toward the cross on the night of Jesus' birth, but we do know that when she and Joseph took Jesus into the Temple to dedicate their son, a devout man named Simeon prophesied that the blessing, which had inspired so much joy, would also have a sharp edge.

> Simeon *blessed them* and said to Mary, his mother:
> "This child is destined to cause the falling and
> rising of many in Israel, and to be a sign that will be
> spoken against, so that the thoughts of many hearts
> will be revealed. *And a sword will pierce your own soul
> too.*"
>
> LUKE 2:34-35, NIV, EMPHASIS ADDED

For more than thirty years, Mary must have meditated on the prophetic word that a sword would pierce her own soul. Were all those years of pondering Simeon's serrated blessing enough to prepare her for what she saw at Golgotha?

Mary was there to witness the awful scene. She was there to see her son stripped and bruised, bleeding and heckled. She was there when the clouds gathered ominously, the sky turned black, and her baby gasped for his last breath. She was there when a sword pierced his side, when a sword pierced her heart. She was there to see the body of her son—the one she nursed, bathed, swaddled, sang to sleep—taken down from the cross. There the woman who once sang *"all generations will call me blessed, for the Mighty One has done great things for me"* must have asked herself if she was now cursed—cursed for bearing the blessing (Luke 1:48-49, NIV). Mary couldn't escape the truth that wrapped within God's greatest blessing was the sharpened edge of a blade.

• • •

When we arrived at the hospital, I thought we were going for a half-hour appointment, not to stay for a week. I hadn't brought anything with me apart from my wallet and my cell phone. During the long hours waiting in the ER, a Muslim family kept glancing at me with concern. Their daughter was in the bed across from my son. She was restless with a high fever, her cheeks flushed, the hair on her forehead damp with sweat.

The mother spoke to me, her voice full of sympathy. "*Geçmiş olsun*," she said—*May the sickness pass*. I replied, "*Rab, sifa versin*"—*May the Lord give health*.

After observing me for hours, she knew I hadn't had anything to eat or drink. Although there was a café in the hospital, my sole purpose had been comforting my boy, and I wasn't about to leave him. The father got up and left the room abruptly. He returned a few minutes later carrying a tray of food—lentil soup, bread, a bottle of water, a pastry—and set it down in front of me. I flushed, not sure how to react. Instinctively, I reached for my wallet, an awkward attempt to offer to pay for the blessing. But he gestured graciously and definitively that there was no chance he'd take a cent. This simple, sincere act of kindness—such a practical blessing—carried me through the painful anxiety of the day.

After we were moved to a hospital room of our own, I had time to ponder our predicament. If you search for bacterial pneumonia on the Internet (something I do not recommend doing if you happen to have a child battling it), you unearth some chilling statistics. UNICEF reports that every year, about 900,000 children five and under die from pneumonia—this infectious disease claims the lives of more young children worldwide than any other sickness.[4] That means that every day, nearly 2,500 mothers bury their little ones—after watching them gradually suffocate from the fluid accumulating in their lungs. It's slow-motion drowning from the inside. Most of these deaths would be preventable if these kids had access to IV fluids, antibiotics, and cleaner environments, like the medication and care my son was receiving.

I think of these thousands of mothers and wonder how they would react to one of Jesus' most perplexing statements: "Blessed are those who mourn" (Matthew 5:4). And I wonder if Mary, standing at the foot of her son's cross, would have been comforted by the thought that "you're blessed when you feel you've lost what is most dear to you" (Matthew 5:4, MSG).

The Beatitudes—the group of eight statements describing those who are blessed, which appears at the beginning of Jesus' Sermon on the Mount (Matthew 5:3-12)—are puzzling in the best of circumstances; sitting in a hospital room with a sick child, they're confounding. How to understand these words that so shatter expectations of what it means to live a blessed life?

Blessed, the word repeated at the beginning of each of Jesus' Beatitudes, is the English translation of the Greek word *makarios.*[5] While *makarios* can be translated blessed, fortunate, or happy, none of these words communicate the full meaning of the concept. It points to the deep and abiding joy people experience from being certain of their relationship with God and of their welcome in his Kingdom. In each Beatitude, there's a present state and a promised future state of blessing. The future dimension is easier for me to grasp, because many of the blessings in the present don't strike me as blessings at all.

Blessed *are* the poor in spirit . . .
Blessed *are* those who mourn . . .
Blessed *are* the meek . . .
Blessed *are* those who hunger and thirst for
   righteousness . . .

Each of these statements is in the present tense. Since when has poverty, mourning, and hunger been a blessing? How do I understand "blessed *are* the poor in spirit" when I know that our hope as believers is to be filled with the Spirit? Isn't a full spirit, not an empty one, a mark of those saved by grace? How do I understand "blessed *are* those who mourn" when Philippians 4:4 exhorts us to rejoice and be glad? Isn't joy, not sorrow, characteristic of those blessed by God?

It's important to note that the Beatitudes are not if/then statements: *If* you are poor in spirit, *then* you'll inherit the Kingdom; *if* you mourn, *then* you'll be comforted; *if* you suffer now, *then* you'll be rewarded in the future. If we read the Beatitudes this way, then we transform them into a set of attitudes and acts that earn us a future blessing. Commenting on Jesus' sermon, Martin Luther emphasized that Jesus *isn't* listing works that will be rewarded with a place in God's Kingdom. We're not called to endure a bleak present so that we can earn a bright future. Rather, Jesus is painting a portrait of a way of being in the world that is only possible if we are already in "a state of grace," already rightly related to God and filled with his spirit.[6]

Various interpretations of Jesus' sermon have been vying for prominence in my mind for weeks. Frustrated by the tangle of readings, I decide to look back to the Old Testament, especially to the prophecies of Isaiah, to make sense of what Jesus might be saying. I pull out a fresh legal pad and write each statement of blessedness on the top its own clean page. Then I start looking for the poor in spirit, the meek, the mourners who are comforted, those hungry for righteousness, the pure in heart, and the peacemakers in the pages of the Old Testament. This approach begins to open up Jesus' teaching to me.

In Luke 4, Jesus inaugurated his public ministry by standing up in the synagogue in his hometown and reading from Isaiah 61: "The Spirit of the Lord is upon me, because he has anointed me to proclaim good news to the poor . . . to proclaim the year of the Lord's favor." And then, while everyone was transfixed by this young man speaking with such authority, he proclaimed, "Today this Scripture has been fulfilled in your hearing" (Luke 4:17-21). Today, right now, *in me*, this Scripture has been fulfilled. If Isaiah 61 was on Jesus' mind in the synagogue, then perhaps there's something in it that will help me understand the statements of blessedness. Reading on from the prophecy Jesus quoted in Nazareth, I find the promise that the one who proclaims the year of the Lord's favor is also the one who comes "to comfort all who mourn" (Isaiah 61:2).

The word *comfort* is a little fuzzy around the edges, so I want to sharpen the definition to understand what Jesus is really saying. *Comfort* is not a common word in the Old Testament,[7] but it's used thirteen times in the book of Isaiah, a full ten of them from chapters 40 to 66, chapters that are brimming with luminous hope—prophecies that were meant to speak powerfully to those living in exile, despairing that they would ever return home.

Comfort, comfort my people,
   says your God.
Speak tenderly to Jerusalem,
   and proclaim to her
that her hard service has been completed,
   that her sin has been paid for . . .

Shout for joy, you heavens;
   rejoice, you earth;
   burst into song, you mountains!
For the LORD *comforts* his people
   and will have compassion on his afflicted ones.

I have seen their ways, but I will heal them;
   I will guide them and restore *comfort* to Israel's
      mourners . . .

As a mother *comforts* her child,
   so will I *comfort* you.

ISAIAH 40:1-2; 49:13; 57:18; 66:13, NIV,
EMPHASIS ADDED

In Isaiah, comfort flows out of God's compassion, and it signals his return that ushers in restoration, redemption, forgiveness of sin, peace, and the advent of a new era defined by joy, gladness, and song. Comfort in Isaiah is the news of the restoration of dashed hope, of miraculous renewal when there had been only despair, of salvation after a dark season of suffering and exile. The comfort promised to the Lord's people is total transformation—from oppressed to free, from broken to restored, from conflict to peace, from exile to being brought near, from exposed to sheltered, from bitter to joyful. Comfort is associated with the return of the Lord, who comes to bring healing and wholeness to those who have been scattered, adrift, shattered.

So when Jesus looked out on the crowd gathered to hear him teach and said, "Blessed are those who mourn, for they will be *comforted*," anyone familiar with the prophecy of Isaiah would have understood the implication—God has returned, and exile is ended. Jesus is saying that when you mourn, you are blessed because the Scripture has been fulfilled, right now, *in me*.

Blessed are those who mourn—No one has the audacity to say these words and mean them except Jesus. Because Jesus isn't saying that mourning is blessing. He isn't saying that despair is happiness. Jesus is saying that if you understand who he is, then your mourning is blessing because he's here with you in it. He's saying that you are blessed because you aren't left alone in grief. God has returned. He is with you. Sorrow *isn't* blessing, but the healing presence of the Lord in the midst of sorrow *is* a profound blessing.

In the most devastating of situations, the places of most excruciating loss, there is only one inexhaustible source of comfort—the presence of God. According to Jesus, the state of being blessed—of deep and abiding happiness and contentment—doesn't mean we'll have freedom from suffering or opposition in the present moment. Rather, "being blessed" is a promise of the experience of supernatural joy in the midst of suffering, of God's presence in the midst of pain, and of the hope that one day, we'll experience blessing in full when God's

Kingdom comes. And it was this dimension of blessing that Mary, who had believed God's word to her from the beginning, knew so well. It was this dimension of blessing she must have experienced when she stood mourning at the foot of the cross.

The Container of the Uncontainable God

On a clear winter day a few years ago, I went with my friend Claire to visit a small chapel near the western edge of the walls that centuries ago protected the city of Constantinople. In the fourth century, the Chora church stood in the open air of a country field, but it's now lost behind a jumble of apartment buildings. The main doors were closed, so we followed a pathway through a modest garden wrapping around the back of the building. We ducked into the side entrance, stepping out of a twenty-first-century city into a fourteenth-century interior. The walls of the two entry hallways leading to a small chapel were awash with mosaics and paintings illustrating the life of Christ and of his mother, Mary.

Standing inside the massive wooden doors that were once the main entrance, I looked up to see a painting of Mary hovering above me. The blue mantle draped over her head and shoulders flowed down over the doorway. Jesus as a young child appeared within a womb-like mandorla centered within Mary's body. The image illustrates that Mary is the passageway, gate, or door through which God came to live among us. It also depicts the awe-inspiring notion that the uncontainable God was once contained within the body of a woman.

Beside the mosaic of Mary, tiny mosaic tesserae spell out three Greek words. Byzantine artists were careful about identifying figures by name in their artwork. So I would expect to find the name Mary, or her honorary title, *Theotokos*, which means God-bearer, associated with the image of her. But not in this church. At Chora, Mary is called the "container of the uncontainable." This playfully paradoxical name for Mary reflects the reality that Byzantine Christians thought of her as the ultimate symbol of one of the central tenets of Christian orthodoxy: The holy, eternal God took on human flesh and became a man. *Incarnation.* By definition, it's not possible for the uncontainable to be contained; and yet, that's precisely what Christians believe happened within the fragile body of a young woman. In Mary, the impossible became possible because the uncontainable God became contained in the tiniest of spaces, a human embryo that dwelt for nine months in the body of a human woman.

We saw in the first chapter of Genesis that God blessed the natural reproductive cycle with fruitfulness, but God blessed Mary uniquely by supernaturally interrupting the flow of the biological process he designed, planting life inside her in the absence of any human touch. The life within her wasn't just any life—it was the life of God himself. And it is right here that I begin to understand how Mary was most blessed. She was blessed because God the Son was near to her—*within her*—in a way he never had been or would be again with anyone in the history of the world.

Faith, like blessing, is oriented toward the future. Mary's whole orientation toward God was one of trust. She believed God's word and allowed it to be accomplished in her life. We know from the hymn Mary sang when she was still young that her vision stretched beyond the immediate present moment. Then she sang, "He [God] has helped his servant Israel, in remembrance of his mercy, as he spoke to our fathers, to Abraham and to his offspring *forever*" (Luke 1:54-55, emphasis added). Mary was looking all the way back to God's blessing of Abraham and all the way forward to eternity.

We moved out of the entry hall and into the chapel. There, over the door, I discovered an image of Mary that was new to me but would have been familiar to Orthodox Christians—an image of Mary's funeral. Her lifeless body rested flat on a slab, the contour of her physical form lost altogether under the stiff, angular folds of her mantle. The disciples congregated around her, mourning her passing. Behind her body, Jesus appeared enveloped in a blaze of light. He stood cradling a baby in his arms.

I wondered about the baby: Who could it be? I asked Claire, who is well-versed in Byzantine iconography, about the meaning of the image. Her answer caught me off guard. She told me that the baby wrapped snug in Christ's embrace represents Mary's soul. The baby symbolizes her spiritual body truly alive in the arms of her son.[8]

I have seen countless paintings of Mary holding Jesus as an infant, but in this mosaic, there is a stunning role reversal— Son embraces mother, lifting her soul to a heavenly home. Mary's body might be spent, but her life is not at an end. Now she will live forever within Christ's glory. Her son has become her Redeemer.

Mary, it turns out, was blessed because she found life in the son she welcomed into the world. The philosopher Søren Kierkegaard suggests Mary "has no need of worldly admiration, any more than Abraham has need of tears, for she was not a heroine, and he was not a hero, but both of them became greater than such, not at all because they were exempted from distress and torment and paradox, but they became great *through* these."[9] Mary was most blessed because she emptied herself, allowing God to fill her with faith and stretch her with a blessing that would become the source of salvation and eternal life for the whole world.

A Blessing for Resting and Waking

The nurse on the night shift just checked my son's vital signs. He's sleeping so soundly that he doesn't stir. The street light filtering through the window falls on his cheek.

A wise friend once reminded me that before we can give blessing, we have to learn to receive blessing. The grace of giving is balanced by opening ourselves to the grace of receiving. Her insight is never truer than in seasons of illness or in long months of grief when our emotional reserves are at their lowest.

When Jesus saw Mary standing at the foot of the cross, he perceived the traumatic loss and the inexpressible grief she was experiencing. And he didn't expect her to face it alone. He blessed her with a son to take his place—his beloved friend John.

> When Jesus then saw His mother, and the disciple whom He loved standing nearby, He said to His mother, "Woman, behold, your son!" Then He said

to the disciple, "Behold, your mother!" From that
hour the disciple took her into his own household.

JOHN 19:26-27, NASB

Jesus gave Mary a blessing of comfort in John. He would
be her protector and companion, someone to comfort and
provide for her. John couldn't take the place of her son Jesus,
but he could help her bear the pain of his loss.

I think back to the practical kindnesses and comfort—*the
blessings*—that have carried us through this week: the friends
who dropped meals by the house when I wasn't around to
cook, a friend who came to sit with Micah one afternoon so I
could take a walk and breathe some fresh spring air, a family
who brought him some games to play while lying in bed. It
would be impossible for me to tease out the material from
the spiritual dimension in these blessings because all of them
were expressions to me of the provision and presence of God
that sustained me during this hospital stay.

I reach over and lay my hand on Micah's forehead. For
a while, I had been so exhausted by the time I got around
to saying prayers with the kids at night that I barely had
the mental energy to put two words together. One night I
prayed,

*May you sleep in the shelter of the shadow of God's wings,
May you wake in the light of his love.*

Now this prayer is becoming like an anchor in our night-
time routine. The psalmist was particularly fond of the image
of hiding beneath God's wings. The metaphor of God's

sheltering wings alludes to God's mercy, faithfulness, protection, favor, and love.[10] David draws on the comfort of the image of God's wings when he's running scared, terrified that King Saul is about to cut his life short. That's the context for Psalm 57, where God's wings of refuge are integrally tied to the experience of his loving mercy: "Be merciful to me, O God, be merciful to me, for in you my soul takes refuge; *in the shadow of your wings I will take refuge*, till the storms of destruction pass by" (verse 1, emphasis added). Sometimes the shadow of God's wings is more than a place to hide; it becomes a place of joyful song: "You have been my help, *and in the shadow of your wings I will sing for joy*" (Psalm 63:7, emphasis added).

The image of God's wings evokes a powerful sense of safety in the midst of danger, uncertainty, and grief. For David, God's wings were his safe haven, and they're mine too. David also used other metaphors to talk about God's protection—he imagined God as a shield, a rock, a warrior.[11] Those images evoke strength and power, but not the warmth and safety of home. The metaphor of finding refuge under God's wings is about more than safety; it speaks to nearness and tenderness. It's about being home next to God.

I'd love to be home right now. I miss tucking my son into his own bed. It looks like tomorrow we'll be able to head home, but until then my son,

May you sleep in the shelter of the shadow of his wings,
May you wake in the light of his love.

chapter 7

BLESSING AROUND THE TABLE

SHARED ABUNDANCE

Bless the crown of the year with your goodness,
for the sake of the poor of your people,
the widow, the orphan, the traveler, the stranger,
and for the sake of us all, who entreat you
and seek your holy name.
For the eyes of everyone wait upon you,
for you give them their food in due season.

AN EGYPTIAN COPTIC CHRISTIAN BLESSING

"**G**od is blessing your work," my friend observed, peering into the kitchen at stacks of cinnamon cookies crowding the countertop. It was Christmas Eve, and I had reluctantly agreed to make at least six dozen cookies for the service at our church.

A couple of years after we moved to Istanbul, we started attending a church in our neighborhood. The petite building tucked between two apartment blocks looked like it would be more at home in the English countryside than in a megacity. The original congregation was made up of an assembly of British expatriates living in the area in the last half of the nineteenth century, during the turbulent twilight of the Ottoman Empire. But over the decades, the original congregation dispersed, until the historic building stood empty and dilapidated. Our congregation offered to lease it and rehabilitate the property. Now the building is once again home to a church.

Sunday worship is usually lively, but no service is as electric as the Christmas Eve service that draws the biggest crowd of the year. The sanctuary is always packed. Faithful members and curious onlookers stand shoulder to shoulder, spilling out of the pews, filling the aisles, pooling in the tiny vestibule. Everyone waits in anticipation for the moment when the lights are extinguished and a single candle is lit to symbolize the birth of Jesus, the Light of the World. The crush of the crowd entirely obstructing the exit is a fire hazard *before* open flame becomes a part of the experience, but afterward, it's a fireman's worst nightmare. As the flame is passed from wick to wick until hundreds of burning candles held aloft by hundreds of congregants illuminate the interior, I find it hard to revel in the wonder of the Incarnation because I'm preoccupied by the concern that someone's hair is about to catch on fire.

A few years back, some of the women in the church started making cookies to serve to those who came to the service. When I was asked to contribute a few batches of cookies, I wanted to say no. I was already exhausted by the flurry of activity in the weeks leading up to the season. I was in the third trimester of what had been a difficult pregnancy. I had already baked what seemed like hundreds of cookies for parties at school and work and as gifts for neighbors. So I wanted to bow out, crawl into bed, and wait for someone to serve me cocoa instead.

But I'm notoriously bad at saying no. And so, on Christmas Eve morning, I found myself looking up recipes for snickerdoodles. I doubled the recipe, hoping that it would make at least sixty cookies.

As I measured and mixed flour and sugar, a dear friend stood leaning against the frame of the kitchen door, observing my progress. Her headscarf was loosely draped over her shoulders, her hair covered by a simple black cotton bonnet underneath. She looked dubious that the dough would stretch so far.

My daughter and I rolled cookie after cookie. Pan after pan kept emerging from the oven. The house smelled like a bakery.

My friend checked in periodically to see what our count was up to. When we reached 120 cookies—twice what I had expected to make—we started laughing in incredulity. There was still a lump of dough left in the mixing bowl, which I wrapped in plastic wrap and placed in the freezer. It stayed there for a month or two, nestled between frozen peas and ice cream, reminding me of the miraculous multiplication of cookies.

An opportunity to share, which I had nearly declined, became one of the greatest sources of joy that holiday. As I packed the cookies into tins, my Muslim friend observed that it was obvious God was blessing my work because he was pleased with my intent to share. I mentioned that the multiplication of the cookies reminded me of a story in the *Injil* (the Gospels) when Jesus fed a crowd of five thousand with a couple of fish and a few loaves of bread.

A Fresh Look at a Familiar Blessing

The miracle of the feeding of the five thousand is so significant, it's the only miracle apart from the Resurrection that is recorded by all four Gospel writers. Matthew, Mark, Luke, and John all remembered the seemingly impossible situation.[1] The disciples were in "a desolate place," at the end of a long day, surrounded by thousands of hungry people. They knew it was impossible to provide for so many. They were ready to send the people away, so they'd be free to retreat and relax. But Jesus looked them in the eyes and challenged them, saying, "You give them something to eat."

The disciples could do the math. Several months' salary wouldn't buy enough bread to feed this crowd. And they knew their natural limitations—they couldn't conjure up bread out of thin air. There was no material solution to the obvious reality that the need exceeded the physical resources available.

But Jesus was not bound by material reality. Instead, he took the resources freely offered—in this case, five loaves and two fish—and he lifted them up to God. Matthew, Mark, and Luke all tell us that Jesus took the bread and fish, looked up to heaven, and "said a blessing over them."

If there's one type of blessing that's familiar to most people, it's the blessing before a meal. The downside of blessings that are so familiar is that they can become routine—prayers we say out of habit, not as true conversation. When I was growing up, our family said a blessing every time we sat down at the table together. "Bless this food to nourish our bodies," my father often prayed. And I always wondered if he thought the words somehow transformed the material composition of the food. I mean, wasn't the meal nourishing whether we blessed it or not?

When my kids gather around our table these days, it's not hard to see their attention is on the food they're about to put in their bellies, not on God. Yesterday at dinner, my littlest reached to sneak a cherry in the middle of the blessing, knocking over her full-to-the-brim cup. As the water spread in a reflective pool over the surface of the smooth wood table-top and dripped onto the carpet underneath, I thanked God I hadn't poured her sticky juice or soda.

Our family prayers before meals don't usually fit a pattern, but lately we've been singing the doxology or a prayer of thanksgiving. When we do *say* a prayer, rather than sing one, we tend to focus on thanksgiving for a good day, for friends and family, for the food, for hands that prepared the food. Our prayers before a meal are steeped in thanksgiving.

I wish I could have heard the words Jesus prayed the day

he lifted up the fish and the bread. I wonder what exactly he said as he blessed the meager meal. One possible reason none of the Gospel writers recorded his words is that it was one they all knew by heart—the *Birkat Hazan*.

The particular words of the Birkat Hazan probably began taking shape during the time of Ezra, when Jews began to return to Jerusalem to rebuild the Temple after a long, painful period of exile in Babylon. But the form of the prayer crystallized during the Talmudic period, when Jewish oral teaching and traditions were written down.[2] As a tradition, blessing God for the provision of food stretched all the way back to the giving of the law on Mount Sinai, where Moses delivered the clear directive: "When you have eaten and are satisfied, *you shall bless the LORD your God* for the good land which He has given you" (Deuteronomy 8:10, NASB, emphasis added). It's pretty clear here that the focus of the blessing isn't the meal itself; it's on the one who provided the meal and the land that produced the crops in the first place. God doesn't call us to bless the food, he asks us *to bless him*, acknowledging that he alone is the source of the blessing. And it occurs to me that our family prayers haven't exactly followed this pattern.

Like all formal Hebrew blessings, the Birkat Hazan begins with a declaration concerning the blessedness of God. The first words mean "Blessed art Thou, Lord our God." In the first century, these words introduced *all* prayer petitions. "The Hebrew passive 'blessed be' signifies that God is the ground or source of all blessings. It also captures the related word *berech* ('knee') to express how we face God in the act of kneeling as creatures in his service."[3]

Blessed art Thou, Lord our God, King of the universe,
who in His goodness, grace, loving kindness, and mercy,
nourishes the whole world.
He gives food to all flesh,
for His loving kindness is everlasting.
In His great goodness, we have never lacked for food;
may we never lack for food, for the sake of His great Name.
For He nourishes and sustains all,
He does good to all,
and prepares food for all His creatures that He created.
Blessed art Thou, Lord, who provides food for all.[4]

This marvelous prayer begins and ends with a blessing of the one who is the source of all blessing. It's a powerful affirmation of God's goodness expressed toward the whole creation through his generous provision. When Jesus raised the bread and fish up to heaven and said a blessing over them, he was affirming God's control over the situation. He was emphasizing that God's sustaining grace provides for all his creatures, day in and day out. And he might have been gently reminding his disciples that the one who "nourishes *the whole world*" every single day is capable of feeding a crowd of a few thousand.

Deuteronomy 8:10 specified that blessing should be said *after* you have eaten and are satisfied. As a result, Jews distinguished between blessings that preceded a meal and those that came at its conclusion. The blessings before eating and drinking are known as *Birkhot Hanehenin*, Blessings of Enjoyment, and they're said for things that bring pleasure.[5] Taken together, the blessings before and after eating infused the entire experience of sharing a meal with the awareness of God's *good* presence. Sharing a meal together is a source of joy, not just because we eat and are filled but because we sit across the table from one another and enjoy each other's company. Satisfaction comes not just from the chicken curry, roasted vegetables, and rice pilaf, or barbeque sliders and fries, but from the fellowship, from pausing to see into the lives of the people sitting across the table.

I've been wondering how we can be more intentional about blessing the Lord when our family prays before a meal. So with the Birkat Hazan in the back of my mind, I jotted down a prayer that we've begun trying to say together some evenings:

> *Blessed are you, Lord God, our Creator and King,*
> *for showing us your kindness in giving us life,*
> *your goodness in giving us food,*
> *and your love in giving us each other.*

We've been saying this prayer on and off for a few weeks, but we still scramble some of the phrases. My littlest is always wiggly, barely paying attention. I wonder if we should abandon this prayer, give up, and go back to the song of thanksgiving. But one night, after reading with her at bedtime, I drop the book on the floor and we pause to say a good-night prayer. My daughter pleads, "Mom, can we say the prayer that God is everything?"

"Which prayer?" I ask, confused. I have no idea what she's talking about.

"You know, Mom, the one that says God *gives everything*."

Tentatively, I ask, "Do you mean the one we say sometimes before dinner?"

A flash of recognition, "Yes, that one, the one we say at dinner!"

And it turns out that she *has* been paying attention. Because if God gives us life, and food, and the love of family and friends, what else is there? That's everything.

Satisfaction and Abundance: Signs That God Walks among Us

Luke tells us that after Jesus blessed the bread, "he broke the loaves and gave them to the disciples to set before the crowd. *And they all ate and were satisfied. And what was left over was picked up, twelve baskets of broken pieces*" (Luke 9:16-17, emphasis added). Luke's delivery is so matter-of-fact that I almost miss the miracle. In this situation, as in so many others, Jesus totally shunned dazzle. The miracle was diffused among his disciples as they mingled with the crowd, serving groups gathered on the hillside. Supernatural provision took place in the context of community as the bread and fish were passed from hand to hand. The bread didn't multiply while sitting in the baskets; it multiplied as it was shared.

Thousands of men, women, and children ate and were satisfied by five barley loaves and two puny fish. No one even seems to have realized that the food multiplied miraculously until *after* they had eaten and began gathering up the leftovers. There's something so low-key about the telling of this miracle that it would be easy to overlook the profound significance at the heart of the event, because for those with eyes to see, it was about much more than a single meal. Matthew, Mark, and Luke note that the people all ate *and were satisfied.*[6] The satisfaction of so many with bread that materialized as if it had rained down from heaven was not just a miracle, it was a *sign*—it signified the presence of the Lord among his people.

During Jesus' final meal with his disciples and closest friends—the night he was arrested, the annual Passover meal—he blessed and broke bread. Then the bread represented his own body. The bread that was blessed, broken, and multiplied as it was passed among a crowd of five thousand prefigured the body of Christ that would be blessed, broken, and multiplied as it would be passed around Sunday after Sunday in churches from the first century up until now.

If there's any doubt that we're meant to make this connection between the feeding of the five thousand and the Lord's Supper, John, the great interpreter of Jesus' ministry, makes sure we don't miss it. In John's Gospel, the day after the miraculous feast, the crowd that had been fed and satisfied came looking for Jesus, who perceived they were driven by a material craving—the hunger in their bellies. "You are seeking me," Jesus said, "because you ate your fill of the loaves." Then he challenged them, saying,

> "The bread of God is he who comes down from heaven and gives life to the world."
>
> They said to him, "Sir, give us this bread always."
>
> Jesus said to them, "*I am the bread of life*; whoever comes to me shall not hunger, and whoever believes in me shall never thirst."
>
> JOHN 6:26, 33-35, EMPHASIS ADDED

There was a physicality about Jesus' statement that disturbed the crowd so much that they bolted. Even those most devoted to Jesus wanted to close their ears: "This is a hard saying;" commented the disciples, "who can listen to it?" (John 6:60). But seen through the prism of the Passover when Jesus blessed the bread and the cup and said, "This is my body, broken for you," these statements take on a profound *symbolic* meaning.[7] Jesus himself is the source of satisfaction. Jesus is the food that endures to eternal life—the ultimate blessing. Jesus is the blessed bread that multiplies as it's shared in community.

In the Old Testament, eating was loaded with meaning. It was associated with the blessing of living in the Promised Land, being in the presence of God, and ultimately, with the hope of living eternally in his Kingdom.[8] Psalm 22, which begins with the despairing words Jesus quoted from the cross—"Why have you forsaken me?"—concludes with the promise of a satisfying meal shared in celebration of God's return. The psalm is a desperate cry for help that culminates in God's decisive response and rescue of the suffering one— redemption that inspires the praise of the nations. One of the signs of God's coming rescue is that "the meek shall *eat and be satisfied*" and those who turn to the Lord will "*eat and worship*" (Psalm 22:26-29, KJV, emphasis added). A feast for the faithful. Eating mingled with worship. Abundance in place of scarcity. Bread appearing miraculously like manna falling from heaven in the desert. The poor eating until they were satisfied. These were all indications of God's blessing, and they testified to God's presence among his people.

In the first chapter of Genesis, we found that multiplication was the original sign of God's blessing—*be fruitful and multiply*—and that same blessing of abundance is repeated here in Jesus' ministry in an unmistakable way. If God blessed through his creative word in Genesis, we should fully expect to see blessing as an integral aspect of Jesus' ministry. If God's blessing was manifested in multiplication, we should expect to find multiplication in Jesus' ministry. If God was revealed as the source of abundant life, then we should expect to find abundance in Jesus' hands. Sure enough, we do.[9]

The One Who Blessed the World

Istanbul is a city that has been put together, broken apart, and reassembled the way my son assembles and disassembles his Legos. Pagan temples were deconstructed to build churches, palaces broken apart to build mosques, collapsed city walls swept away to make way for high-rise apartments. For at least two thousand years (and maybe all the way back to the Bronze Age), the building blocks of the city ended up integrated into some new configuration. Some days, I walk out the door and imagine this history churning under the layers of asphalt—the stories of the lives lived here stifled by so many tons of rebar and cement.

But despite centuries of reconfiguration of the city surrounding it, the *Hagia Sophia*—the Church of the Holy Wisdom—still stands. Its longevity seems miraculous, given that the other two churches previously built on the site didn't have nearly so enduring a presence. The first burned to the ground in the fifth century after a golden-tongued preacher, John Chrysostom, was exiled from the capital. His loyal congregants are suspected of igniting their own church in protest. The cathedral built on the ashes of the first basilica burned too, a casualty of the Nika riot, a clash between rival groups that spilled out of the nearby Hippodrome where chariot races were held. The destruction gave the emperor Justinian I the opportunity to commission one of the most ambitious building projects of the ancient world, a cathedral crowned by a massive fluted dome, the likes of which had never been seen. On December 27, 537, when the church was consecrated, the overall impression it gave those gathered for worship was that heaven had come down to earth.[10] Over the centuries, the Hagia Sophia has weathered earthquakes, war, and occupation, the transition from a church to mosque, and then from mosque to museum. But it still stands, inviting me to admire its lovely bones, porphyry columns, and soaring heights. Today, I'm here with a friend.

Pausing in the doorway leading from the outer to the inner *narthex*, a long outer hallway that leads to the massive doors entering the sanctuary, I look above the imperial door, where the emperor would have removed his crown before entering the church to worship. I gaze at a mosaic of an emperor bowing down before a regal-looking Christ seated on a jeweled throne. In his left hand, Jesus holds a book inscribed with a blessing: "Peace be upon you, I am the light of the world." His right hand is raised in a sign of the blessing of peace.

Everyone who visits this church is greeted by blessing— one in words, the other in gesture. It's not the last time I'll see evidence of blessing. In the apse of the church, distinguished by the central semidome that would have commanded the attention of all gathered to worship, Christ sits as a small child on Mary's lap. His right hand, again, is raised in blessing.

I climb the stone ramp to the upper gallery, running my fingers over exposed brick and broad bands of mortar. There I find mosaics from the eleventh century, and again, Jesus' right hand is raised in blessing. Leaving the southern gallery, I pause before another image of Christ made in the late thirteenth century, after crusaders from Europe abandoned the city they had plundered and burned to the ground. This mosaic is badly damaged, but even so, the flesh tones of Jesus' face feel fresh and lifelike, rendered in a naturalistic style that predated the Renaissance. This mosaic might have been inspired by one of the earliest known portraits of Christ—a painted icon preserved in Saint Catherine's Monastery in Sinai, Egypt. In this image, too, Jesus' right hand is raised in blessing.

Leaving the dim interior of the church, I sit down on the marble steps under a portico, thinking how different these images are from the pictures of Jesus I grew up seeing. There has always been a dynamic relationship between the way images shape our beliefs and the way they reflect them. For Christians through the centuries, images of Christ have always carried theological meaning. So it's significant that in Christian images from the sixth century all the way up to the Renaissance, Jesus was almost always depicted with his right hand raised in a gesture of blessing. For more than a millennium, when Christians imagined Jesus, they pictured him as *Pantocrator*, God Almighty, *the source of blessing for the whole world.*

Commissioned with a Blessing

Reading the accounts of Jesus' life in the Gospels, I begin to realize why early Christian artists so often depicted Jesus in the act of blessing. When people brought their children to Jesus, he took them in his arms and *blessed* them. Before breaking bread, Jesus blessed God for providing the meal. When his disciples left for their first mission, Jesus sent them with a blessing of peace. After the Resurrection, Jesus greeted his disciples with a blessing. And the disciples' last glimpse of Jesus in the flesh was while he was in the act of blessing them. As he ascended into the heavens, he blessed those gathered to witness what must have been an awe-inspiring departure: "When he [Jesus] had led them out to the vicinity of Bethany, he lifted up his hands and *blessed* them. While he was *blessing* them, he left them and was taken up into heaven" (Luke 24:50-51, NIV, emphasis added).[11]

In Luke's description of Jesus' ascension, the word translated "bless" is the Greek word *eulogein*.[12] It's the root of our English word *eulogy*, which I primarily associate with speeches at funerals and the scent of faded lilies. But in the classical sense, *eulogein* had a much broader application, meaning to praise or to speak well of someone. In the New Testament, though, *eulogein* is used in the classical Greek sense only once; in every other instance, the concept behind the word is the Hebrew *berakah*—the powerful conception of blessing we encountered in the Old Testament that meant a vital power essential for life.[13]

When we find the word *bless* in the Gospels, then, it carries with it all the weight of blessing in God's history with his people, particularly the covenant with Abraham, and the anticipated future state of blessing in the prophetic tradition. It means not just to speak well of someone but "to call God's grace upon someone."[14] When Jesus blessed his disciples as he ascended, he was calling God's grace, goodness, and power upon them. I wonder if, perhaps, Jesus as the great High Priest was reciting the priestly blessing of Numbers 6: "May Yahweh bless you and protect you."

Looking for insight into the meaning of Jesus' final blessing, I flip through Claus Westermann's study, *Blessing in the Bible and the Life of the Church*. No one has investigated the subject of blessing in the Bible more thoroughly than Westermann. He reminds me that the historical context for Jesus' blessing during the Ascension doesn't fit the priestly blessing. He suggests that the better parallel is a traditional blessing given at parting. Westermann explains:

> The one who gives the blessing imparts a power that remains with those he leaves behind, and this power maintains the ties between those who are separated from each other. The specific meaning in this special situation where the Lord parts from his community lies in the fact that it is this crucified and risen Lord who is leaving his blessing and his peace behind with his community . . . by bestowing his blessing he is leaving power with them.[15]

So then, Jesus' parting blessing during his ascension goes hand-in-hand with his commission. The power of his blessing carries his followers out into the world with a mission fueled by the power of his Spirit living in and through them. This reading squares perfectly with the picture we get in John's Gospel, where Jesus' blessing of peace dovetails immediately with his sending of the disciples after his resurrection—"Peace be with you. As the Father has sent me, even so I am sending you" (John 20:21). Just as Abraham had been called out to become a blessing for all the families of the earth, now the disciples will take up that mantle, carrying the blessing of Christ with them.

In fact, the integral tie between blessing and mission emerged even earlier in Jesus' ministry. When he sent out seventy-two of his followers to go ahead of him into the towns he expected to visit, he sent them out with a specific blessing—the blessing of peace. "Whatever house you enter," he said, "first say, '*Peace be to this house.*' If a man of peace is there, your peace will rest on him; but if not, it will return to you" (Luke 10:5-6, NASB, emphasis added).

In the context of a commission, the blessing of peace isn't incidental direction. It's not icing on the proverbial cake of ministry in the world. Blessing is part of the way Jesus' followers reflect his character and embody his presence. After all, in Ephesians, Paul tells us that Jesus was the one who "came and *preached peace* to you who were far off and peace to those who were near" (Ephesians 2:17, emphasis added). Paul's testimony reflects the earlier prophecy of Zechariah, who envisioned the Messiah preaching peace to the nations:

Behold, your king is coming to you;
He is just and endowed with salvation . . .

> *And He will speak peace to the nations;*
> And His dominion will be from sea to sea.
>
> ZECHARIAH 9:9-10, NASB, EMPHASIS ADDED

Zechariah wasn't the only prophet who saw peace as an essential aspect of the return of the Lord. Isaiah, too, often spoke of peace, prophesying the arrival of the *Prince of Peace*, who would establish a *government of peace* (Isaiah 9:6-7). He envisioned a time when God's Spirit would be poured out upon us from on high and "the work of righteousness will be peace" (Isaiah 32:16-18, NASB). And he recognized that God would one day send out messengers to tell others of this marvelous peace: "How lovely on the mountains are the feet of him who brings good news, *Who announces peace*" (Isaiah 52:7, NASB, emphasis added).

Jesus came preaching peace; he came bearing a blessing of peace, and he asked those who follow him to do the same. The blessing of peace is not peripheral to evangelism; it's a way of communicating the goodness of finding peace with God through his Son. If Jesus is the Prince of Peace who speaks peace to the nations, then the message of those who follow him should be suffused with the blessing of peace that flows out of the steadfast love of the Lord seeking reconciliation with his children.

I think of Jesus' conversation with his disciples around the Passover table the night before his crucifixion. "*Peace* I leave with you," he said, "*My peace* I give to you; not as the world gives do I give to you" (John 14:27, NASB, emphasis added). The peace Jesus gave his disciples that night was given to share. They wouldn't stay huddled together in that upper room enjoying the peace of the Lord in safety and security. They would go out into the world, inviting others to enjoy this divine peace. "Blessed," Jesus said, "are the peacemakers," for they are the sons and daughters of God (Matthew 5:9, author's paraphrase).

"Go in peace . . ."

I live in a part of town where I can walk to get things done. I walk to the market, the pharmacy, the bakery, the butcher, the dry cleaner, the coffee shop, the book store. You get the picture; I burn up the sidewalks.

On my way to the grocery store to pick up some chicken for dinner, I pass a father and his young daughter. They're sitting on a scrap of cardboard and begging. I try not to meet his desperate gaze. I quicken my pace and breeze right by. I don't give them a blessing—I don't say or do anything at all. Even in my rush, I can't help but notice that his daughter must be about the age of my youngest. And I'm aware that she and her father are most likely Syrian.

Millions of Syrian refugees have flooded over Turkey's porous southern border attempting to salvage what's left of their lives after their homes and businesses were leveled by bombs or occupied by foreign fighters. Turkey has provided camps and services for millions of Syrian refugees, absorbing more vulnerable families than any other country in the world. But still, more arrive every day, overwhelming those providing services, food, and shelter. Many are left on the streets, hemmed in by closed borders and a sea that has already swallowed thousands undertaking the crossing.

Walking up to the market, I'm distracted, my heart a few steps behind my body, my mind back there on the sidewalk. I browse shelves stocked abundantly, and I start tossing items into a basket—carrots, onions, a loaf of bread . . . oh, and I need chicken. I came for chicken.

But I feel a gnawing sense that maybe I'm not here just for chicken. I can't walk out of this store with my bulging bags of groceries and pass by that hungry family sitting on the sidewalk. I could avoid them. I could cross the street, dash home, and eat well. But at the moment, I don't feel hungry. The warning in the book of James needles my heart: "If a brother or sister is poorly clothed and lacking in daily food, and one of you says to them, 'Go in peace, be warmed and filled,' without giving them the things needed for the body, what good is that?" (James 2:15-16).

James identifies the vital connection between spiritual blessing and material provision. To speak gracious words while withholding available provision from someone in need is no blessing at all. Our actions should embody the content of our blessings; otherwise, our words are hollow shells. They have form but no life. There can be no *shalom*—peace, well-being, and wholeness—where there is hunger, destitution, and homelessness. Those who pray for peace, suggests James, better actively try to generate it.

I walk back to the entrance and pick up another basket. I fill it with staples—rice, red lentils, oil, cheese, beef sausage, milk, bread, butter, honey, raisins. I add a few treats like chocolate, hazelnuts, sesame, and pistachio brittle. I grab a toothbrush like the one my daughter uses and a pair of socks from a bin near the cash register. Then I retrace my steps, walking back the way I came. When I approach the father and his daughter, I kneel down, handing her the bags.

Perhaps I should have said something to bless her, but I don't speak at all. Honestly, I'm blinking back tears because in the depths of my being, I know this bag of groceries isn't enough. This isn't the blessing this family truly needs. They need an end to the war that drove them from their home. They need a refuge, a safe place, access to education, and meaningful work. They need enduring political peace and eternal spiritual peace. But maybe this small offering is a taste of God's good blessing like the broken pieces of bread and fish that once multiplied on a hillside in Galilee.

May the empty be filled,
the hungry eat well,
the thirsty drink deep,
and the wounded in spirit be restored,
as those far off are brought near.

May the full live open handed,
the mended heal,
the satisfied provide,
as those comfortable at the table welcome others to the
     meal,
where bread broken multiplies,
and cups overflow.

chapter 8

BLESSING EVEN ENEMIES

THE ARENA OF GRACE

Love through me, Love of God,
Make me like Thy clear air
Through which unhindered, colours pass
As though it were not there.

AMY CARMICHAEL, *TOWARD JERUSALEM*

When Roman soldiers marched Polycarp into the arena in the seaside town of Smyrna, I wonder if the elderly pastor recalled the words he had written years earlier: "If we suffer for His name's sake, let us glorify Him."[1] Bound like a criminal and jeered by the crowd, Polycarp was about to discover whether or not he could live the words he had once penned. As a young man, Polycarp had been schooled in the Christian faith by the apostle John. He must have been a good student, because his faithfulness to the gospel was borne out in an exceedingly long ministry and, ultimately, in an exceedingly public death.

A few years ago, the demolition of a row of shanty houses in the Turkish city of İzmir unearthed the walls of the ruined arena where Polycarp was burned. Since then, 175 buildings have been demolished in an effort to uncover the coliseum that archeologists believe once held as many as 16,000 people.[2] In the second century, when pagan temples still dominated the landscape, occasional waves of persecution surged through the empire. The execution of notable Christians who refused to offer incense to the old gods became sport and spectacle, another game to feature in the arena of the empire.

Evarestus, the scribe who wrote down the details of Polycarp's martyrdom in the last half of the second century, left us the earliest surviving authentic account of a Christian martyrdom outside Stephen's murder recorded in the book of Acts. And like Stephen in the face of a furious mob, Polycarp held calmly to the faith that had sustained him his whole life. When asked to disown Christ, he memorably replied, "Eighty and six years have I served Him, and He has done me no wrong. How then can I blaspheme my King and my Savior?"

That understated answer sealed his fate. He climbed up onto the pyre after removing his shoes. Then soldiers set the wood on fire. It was said that as the flames blazed around him, "the fire took on the shape of a hollow chamber, like a ship's sail when the wind fills it, and formed a wall around about the martyr's figure." To put it somewhat less poetically, Polycarp's body refused to burn. When fire failed them, the soldiers stabbed the good bishop.

Evarestus recounts Polycarp's martyrdom with a poetic flair that no doubt made it memorable, but it is the less spectacular details—the ones that could almost go unnoticed— that are most telling about the character of this man willing to follow Jesus into an inferno.

In the weeks before Polycarp was arrested, Evarestus reports, eleven Christians had been paraded into the arena to die in gruesome ways. So when the crowd began chanting Polycarp's name, his friends knew they'd better hide their bishop. They stashed him in a nondescript farmhouse outside of town, hoping he could ride out the storm among the fields and olive groves. When his hideout was discovered, they moved him again.

Polycarp was asleep in an attic when the soldiers came knocking. To their astonishment, he didn't try to resist arrest, spit in their faces, or curse their names; instead, he insisted on serving them a meal. He asked the men with their hands on the hilts of their swords to sit down at his table. He gave instructions that they "be given all the food and drink they wanted." Polycarp stood praying as they ate. In the face of his composure and grace, the men who were there to facilitate his execution "began to regret this expedition against a man so old and saintly."[3]

An uncharitable reading might suggest the dinner was a delay tactic, a way of forestalling death. But it's much more likely that Polycarp was living out Paul's practical directive that echoed Jesus' teaching on blessing even enemies: "If your enemy is hungry, feed him; if he is thirsty, give him something to drink" (Romans 12:20).

When I read *The Martyrdom of Polycarp*, it's this moment I love the most—the elderly pastor at prayer as he shares bread with his enemies. The clamor of the circus falls away in the face of this quiet grace. Through this generous gesture, Polycarp embodied the most difficult of all of Jesus' teachings: loving those who hate and blessing those who curse. Polycarp could stand fearlessly facing death in the arena of the empire because he believed his soul was safe in the arena of grace. He could forgive those who shackled him because he worshiped a Savior who had forgiven the soldiers who nailed him to the tree. He could offer his persecutors a meal because he knew Jesus had served breakfast to a disciple who had betrayed him. Polycarp gave mercy because he had received mercy. He blessed because he had been blessed.

The Arena of the Empire: Reciprocity and Retribution

We saw in the last chapter that in so many ways, Jesus' practice of blessing was continuous with the understanding of blessing in the Old Testament. The way he blessed children, blessed meals, blessed upon arriving and departing were all perfectly in step with how blessing had developed over centuries in the life of Israel. But Jesus' approach to blessing also broke with tradition. In some significant ways, his understanding of blessing was radically innovative. And it is in his teaching on blessing in the Sermon on the Mount in Matthew 5–7 and in the parallel sermon in Luke 6 that we first realize how radical his teaching was. Jesus totally disrupted expectations regarding who the people of God are obligated to bless. It's in this discontinuity with tradition that the contours of Jesus' mission begin to emerge most clearly.

"You have heard that it was said, 'You shall love your neighbor and hate your enemy.' But I say to you . . ." (Matthew 5:43-44). *You have heard that it was said*: With this statement, Jesus directly acknowledges the crowd's expectations (and ours) for the way relationships work in real life. Reciprocity rules our world. It's the grease that oils the gears of relationships. It's instinctual, possibly even intrinsic to human nature. Extricating ourselves from the comfort and stability of this efficient system sounds crazy, maybe even self-destructive. We all intuitively understand that there's often an underlying motive of self-interest in being good to the people who are good to us. But the rule of reciprocity that often encourages acts of generosity and kindness also has the potential to cement cycles of violence when reciprocity devolves into retribution. You cut me off in traffic, I'll tailgate you until you regret it. You take credit for my great idea at work, I'll undercut your authority with the team and bad-mouth you behind your back. You post a sarcastic comment at my expense on social media, I'll reply with a burn that'll make you regret it.

Retribution may be law in the arena of the empire, but that isn't the social space Jesus calls us into. In the arena of grace, Jesus' rule transcends retribution. Self-interested love expressed in blessing *only* those who bless us in return may be natural, but it's not at all like the love God invites us to experience and share. Jesus challenges: "If you love those who love you, what benefit is that to you? For even sinners love those who love them. And if you do good to those who do good to you, what benefit is that to you?" (Luke 6:32-33). With these rhetorical questions, Jesus is sketching the contours of the "Christian counter-culture," a community of people who should be known by their love *for all*, their goodness *to all*, their prayers *for all*, their blessing *of all*.[4]

The Arena of Grace

> Love your enemies, do good to those who hate you, bless those who curse you, pray for those who abuse you. To one who strikes you on the cheek, offer the other also, and from one who takes away your cloak do not withhold your tunic either.
>
> LUKE 6:27-29

The main thing that jumps out at me when I read this passage is that each one of these statements is an emphatic command. *Love, do good, bless, pray for*—this rule is addressed to everyone who follows Jesus. Obedience is not optional.

Each of these commands is inseparable from the others, but love is the ground of them all. Blessing those who curse is love expressed in words, while doing good is love expressed in action. Jesus is saying that the entire orientation of the self—in thought, word, deed, and prayer—should be focused on the good of others, *even* our enemies. Collectively, these commands point to the reality that for Christians, hatred, malice, retribution, and curse are forbidden fruit.

Jesus' teaching on loving enemies was so unexpected, so surprising, and so revolutionary that it "has rightly been described as *the most characteristic saying of Jesus.*"[5] "Bless those who curse"—with these words, Jesus lays the foundation for an entirely new sort of arena. It's nothing like the Roman arena, where retribution was sporting fun, and spectators and players were encouraged to vent their prejudice and rage—nothing like the arena of the empire, where strength trumps weakness and the merciless rule. As Jesus begins to frame the moral orientation of those who follow in his way, he's constructing an alternative arena—the arena of grace.

Blessing those who curse is taking a stand within a totally different playing field. It is inviting others into a space where forgiveness takes the place of vengeance, where kindness answers insult, where stalwart goodness responds to impulsive assault, where invincible goodwill overcomes bitterness, where the merciless are met with mercy.

This is a strange arena to a world where aggression tends to be met either by a defensive response—blow for blow, insult for insult—or by retreat from confrontation. Our minds and bodies are hardwired toward fight or flight—but Jesus calls us to override our adrenaline-fueled biological systems. When we begin to suspect that this way of living is impossible, we have to remind ourselves that Jesus is not asking us to do something that he has not already done himself.

Jesus is not only the architect of the arena of grace but also the portal into it and the first to take up residence within this unnatural—this *supernatural*—way of being. In Romans, Paul reminds us that Christ demonstrated his love by dying for us *while we were still God's enemies* (5:6-10). And Peter ties Jesus' call to love our enemies and to bless those who curse to the pattern Jesus set in his own death on the cross: "When he was reviled, he did not revile in return; when he suffered, he did not threaten" (1 Peter 2:23). From the cross, Jesus showed us what his teaching looks like when it's put into practice, and he called us to pattern our lives after his example. "*To this you were called*," says Peter, to "not repay evil for evil or reviling for reviling, but on the contrary, bless" (1 Peter 3:9, author's paraphrase, emphasis added).

But I have to ask: Is it healthy to bless those who curse? Is it right to love those who wound? Do I have the strength of soul to meet an enemy as if they could become "a fellow heir of the grace of life?"[6]

I don't know if I can live this way. But I know I've seen it done.

• • •

I met Matthew[7] in Bulgaria, when I sat across from him at my friend Audrey's kitchen table on a Sunday afternoon. Between us was a glass casserole dish filled with *banitsa*, a savory pastry stuffed with mild white cheese. Audrey was from Texas, so her version wasn't exactly traditional—she added at least a half-dozen eggs and a generous helping of melted butter. As a result, the crust was a beautiful golden caramel color, crispy and irresistible. Matthew, a

Sudanese refugee, loved her home-style cooking as much as I did.

Audrey's husband, James, pastored an international church, and after Sunday service, they hosted lunch in their apartment for anyone who cared to come. This afternoon, I had shown up, along with a handful of other takers, including Matthew. It was easy to see that his life had been hard. One of his eyes was scarred, and he walked with a noticeable limp. I didn't have the courage to ask about the origin of these wounds. Instead, we talked about my family and the bitter Bulgarian winters. An African who had never seen snow before he was transplanted to the Balkans, he couldn't get used to the weather. Even after a couple of years, he hadn't acclimated—he said he felt chilled most of the time.

A few months later, I watched from my perch in the balcony of a local Baptist church as Matthew, favoring his good leg, slowly climbed the steps to the pulpit. He was there to share the story I'd been too timid to ask about. He described an attack outside his family home when a group of soldiers stole his sister and shot his father. He cradled his dad in his arms while the life drained out of him. Then the soldiers dragged Matthew away to prison. His limp was the result of permanent nerve damage caused by electroshock torture. They beat him so severely, they destroyed the vision in one of his eyes.

A priest who occasionally visited the facility where Matthew was being held helped him escape. He walked across the desert to the Mediterranean Sea, a perilous journey fueled mostly by rage and a commitment to one day kill the men who murdered his father. He applied for refugee status and was offered a place as a student in Bulgaria. There, he met a preacher who talked about Jesus and his teaching on loving your enemies—an idea that struck him as ridiculous and infuriating.

Matthew confronted James after a service in which James had preached about the Sermon on the Mount. He was convinced it was utterly impossible to love the men who executed his father, took his sister, and wrecked his body. He wanted vengeance, not forgiveness. But over months of conversation and study, Jesus' message started to erode his hatred. Matthew chose to follow the way of the cross, fully understanding that that decision meant forgiving and loving the men who had taken everything from him.

Forgiveness, Matthew said, freed him from hatred. He had discovered a new reason for living—not vengeance, but mission. So when his studies were over, he planned to return to the place of his deepest sorrow and find the men who killed his father to tell them about the love that had saved him, because he believed it had the power to save them too.

Only in the arena of grace could a man walk straight toward death with a message of life. Seeing this brand of love in action is arresting—it literally arrests the cycle of violence that tends to spiral out of control in the eye-for-an-eye, tooth-for-a-tooth economy.

Extending mercy to the merciless may seem nonsensical because it's self-sacrificial, not self-protective, but that's precisely what makes it supernatural. It's not possible to love like this in our own power, only through the power of God's Spirit alive in us. This love isn't instinctual; it's born of the supernatural presence of God in us. We don't enter the arena of grace through our own strength, but only by humbling ourselves to the ground.

The Most Inclusive Blessing Imaginable

Even as I reflect on Matthew's testimony, I'm nursing a lingering concern that by blessing those who curse, I might be implicitly approving of bad behavior. If I extend love to those who do and say things that hurt me and others, am I sanctioning their destructive acts?

In Western culture, the concept of giving a blessing is often synonymous with the idea of giving approval. Asking for a blessing can be a way of asking for permission or acceptance. So, for instance, when a guy wants to marry a girl and he asks for her father's blessing, in essence, he's asking for approval. Does the father *permit* him to marry his daughter? In this context, the father's blessing signals his approval of the match.

This understanding of blessing often mingles with what we think the call to bless means in Scripture. But here's the thing: In the context of the Sermon on the Mount, the call to love enemies *doesn't* mean approving of immoral behavior or character; instead, blessing is goodness poured out regardless of the worthiness of the recipient. That's why Jesus says blessing those who curse reflects the phenomenal generosity of God who is even "kind to the ungrateful and wicked" (Luke 6:35, NIV). In this context, blessing, Jesus shows us, operates in the arena of common grace.

God's blessing is an expression of common grace before it ever reflects saving grace (a dimension of blessing we'll explore in the next chapter).[8] When Jesus calls us to bless our enemies, he calls us into a ministry that reflects the grace of a God who showers goodness even on those who don't deserve it. To bless those who curse is to extend *unmerited* favor, *undeserved* mercy, *unearned* grace. God blesses those who long for his blessing and the scoundrels who don't. He sends rain on the rulekeepers and the rulebreakers, on the thankful and the unthankful, on the hardworking and on the lazy cheats, on the devoted and on the indifferent. God blesses indiscriminately, and he asks us to do the same. And if you want to be like him, says Jesus, "Be merciful, even as your Father is merciful" (Luke 6:36).

Fear of condoning sinful behavior often causes Christians to withhold blessing from those we perceive to be living outside of God's grace. But Jesus challenges this stance. He says that there's no one—*no one at all*—from whom Christians should withhold blessing. If we're called to bless *even* enemies—*even* those who insult, deride, and persecute followers of Jesus—then there is no one we're not called to bless. So that means we're called to bless those we get along with and those we don't. We're called to bless those whose political views align with ours, and those whose don't. We're called to bless those within the walls of our congregations and those without. We're called to bless people in all walks of life everywhere along the social spectrum, because to bless in this inclusive way reflects the common grace and good character of God, who "causes his sun to rise on the evil and the good, and sends rain on the righteous and the unrighteous" (Matthew 5:45, NIV). When we live this way, we show ourselves to be children of God (Luke 6:35-36).

When we love this way, we share in Christ's suffering. As Dietrich Bonhoeffer said in his classic *The Cost of Discipleship*, "Perfect, all-inclusive love is the act of the Father, it is also the act of the sons of God as it was the act of the only-begotten Son," and "The love for our enemies takes us along the way of the cross and into fellowship with the Crucified."[9]

Loving the haters isn't accepting bad behavior; it's a way of resisting it. Blessing our enemies isn't condoning aggression; it's a way of subverting it. Blessing those who persecute isn't celebrating violence; it's a way of breaking the cycle of hurt. Remember that blessing is always oriented toward seeing a future good realized in someone's life. So that means that we don't accept the evil of the present when we bless our enemies; instead, we're begging the Lord to transform everyone involved, to work through the hard and make it good, to work within the sin-stained dividing lines and bring reconciliation.

In our discussion of Jacob blessing his sons, we saw how he censured the violent anger of Simeon and Levi in the context of a family blessing because calling out their destructive behavior was for the protection and good of the community as a whole. Similarly, there may be instances when we feel compelled to confront violence, abuse, or injustice for the sake of protecting victims and promoting lasting peace. In these situations, blessing may take on a critical prophetic edge, but the internal attitude that motivates our words and actions must be love, not hate. Our aim should be redemption, not damnation.

It takes extraordinary grace to be insulted and return a blessing. It takes extraordinary generosity to be taken from and offer to give more. It takes extraordinary restraint to receive a blow and turn the other cheek. It takes extraordinary resolve to look evil in the face and speak truth in love. But it is precisely this extraordinary grace, generosity, restraint, and resolve that changes the world.

Subverting Evil with Blessing

One January midnight in 1956, in the middle of the Montgomery bus boycott, the phone rang in Martin Luther King Jr.'s home. While his wife, Coretta, and newborn baby girl, Yolanda Denise, were sleeping nearby, he listened as an anonymous caller threatened to blow up his house if he didn't leave town. Three days later, the caller made good on his promise. King was at a meeting when a bomb tossed onto the front porch exploded, terrorizing the family, who fled to the back of the house, narrowly escaping harm.

In the aftermath of the attack, an armed crowd of King's supporters assembled on the lawn in front of his home. If peaceful protests inspired this sort of vicious response targeting women and children, then maybe it was time to meet explosives with firearms—the crowd called for retaliation. But King raised his hand and spoke, calling them to peace, reminding them of Jesus' way. "We cannot solve this problem through retaliatory violence," he counseled. "We must meet violence with non-violence. . . . We must love our white brothers no matter what they do to us. We must make them know we love them. . . . Jesus still cries out in words that echo across the centuries: 'Love your enemies; bless them that curse you; pray for them that despitefully use you.' *This is what we must live by.*"[10]

That he was able to utter these words with conviction on the night his family was very nearly murdered seems a superhuman feat of love to me. But this orientation to love didn't emerge in King spontaneously in a moment of crisis; it was an attitude he had been cultivating over years of prayer, immersion in the Scripture, and contemplation of Jesus' ministry, which had instilled in him a resolve to "not be overcome by evil, but overcome evil with good" (Romans 12:21).

This sort of love isn't weak; it's strong. It looks hatred in the eye and refuses to stoop to its level. It avoids both external violence and what King called the "internal violence of the spirit."[11] Blessing in response to cursing and seeking reconciliation rather than retaliation has a powerful potential to effect change. Less than a year after the attack on King's home, buses in Montgomery were integrated. The same year, in a speech to the First Annual Institute on Nonviolence and Social Change, King expounded on the particular kind of love that characterizes love toward enemies:

> *Agape* means nothing sentimental or basically affectionate. It means understanding, redeeming good will for all men. It is an overflowing love which seeks nothing in return. It is the love of God working in the lives of men. When we rise to love on the *agape* level we love men not because we like them, not because their attitudes and ways appeal to us, but because God loves us.[12]

No one has embodied this brand of love more fully than Jesus. Agape love was on full display when Jesus forgave his enemies from the cross. This divine love involves surrendering self to redeem others. And it is in this total orientation of self that Jesus' teaching becomes excruciatingly hard, because it's not enough to bless through gritted teeth. It's not enough to mumble a few kind words while harboring anger in our hearts. We have to mean the blessing. We have to will the truth of the words we say with our whole being, even when, especially when, we do not naturally feel them. "Prayer without intention," said the Jewish rabbis in Jesus' day, "is like a body without a soul."[13]

The battle to forgive, to love, to bless doesn't begin with what we say and do—it begins with what we believe and pray. Genuine desire for the good of those who I sense do not want good for me only grows out of the understanding and acceptance that God has forgiven me. That's the reason Jesus wraps up his teaching on blessing those who curse by observing that what we say flows out of the abundance of our hearts. "For each tree is known by its own fruit," Jesus observes, "For figs are not gathered from thornbushes, nor are grapes picked from a bramble bush. The good person out of the good treasure of his heart produces good, and the evil person out of his evil treasure produces evil" (Luke 6:44-45). Prayer is where this gardening begins. In prayer, the Holy Spirit cultivates the soil of our hearts, uprooting seedlings of bitterness and pruning away pride that evolves so easily into prejudice. In the moments we meet God, confessing our hatred, praying good for those who have wounded us, we begin to sow seeds of peace. "A blessing does not erase the difficult nor abolish it; but it does reach deeper to draw out the hidden fruit of the negative. The old patterns do not evaporate, but become transformed under the persuasion of the soul's new affection."[14]

Who are my enemies? The flip side of this question is to ask, *When and to whom have I been an enemy?* I know that as often as I've felt insulted, I've been guilty of insulting. As often as I've felt devalued, I've devalued others. As often as I've felt sidelined, I've excluded others. It's an awful truth that the people who are most beloved are often the ones who wound us the most deeply. Mistakes, misunderstandings, harsh words, or betrayal can drive a wedge between family members and close friends. But Jesus shows us the way through this cold season of separation. Before forgiving others, we receive his forgiveness. Before loving, we receive his love. Before blessing, we receive his blessing. Then we open our hearts to give the way we've received.

How to become the sort of person who blesses without bounds, who loves even in the presence of hatred, who overcomes evil with good? How to begin finding my footing in the arena of grace? As with all hard things, I know I have to start small. So I start by praying for the people who irritate me—people like the taxi driver who ripped me off, or the woman who shoved past me in line at the grocery store, or the colleague whose condescension was insulting. I can't know the complex dynamics at play in their lives, what motivated them in the moment. But I can ask the Lord to bless them and speak to them through whatever pain or pressure is afflicting them.

And then I try to pray blessing for those who are nearer. I think of painful conversations I've stayed awake at night replaying over and over in my mind. I think of a friend whose criticism left a raw wound for months. I think of the bitterness I've harbored toward those who have misunderstood and abused those I love. I pray for God to forgive me for holding on to these hurts and to enable me to release them to him for healing. Mostly, I pray for the peace of his presence to close the distance between me and these loved ones, because the arena of grace is best recognized by the reconciliation that happens within its translucent walls.

Then I call to mind the men who kidnapped my friend.

I remember the last evening I spent with her—this gentle woman with a radiant smile who was equipping women with skills that would enable them to support their families. It was early January, not long after we boxed up all our Christmas decorations. Chicken curry was simmering on the stove, and a pot of rice was steaming. I walked around the corner from the kitchen to the dining room and saw her sitting with her legs crossed on our white wool carpet, playing with my daughter. She was the sort of woman who got down on the floor to be at eye level with kids so that they felt seen.

A week later, she returned to the remote area where she lived. She emailed a note of thanks and asked for my curry recipe. I hadn't even had time to respond when the news broke that a group of armed men had surrounded her car one morning when she was on her way to work. She has never been seen again. I can still run my fingers over the delicate stitches on the embroidered silk pillows made by the women she served—a beautiful remnant of a life well lived.

For years, there's been a stubborn knot in my heart. I've refused to pray for the men who stole her away. I've cast them in my mind as faceless masked monsters—incarnations of hate, not bearers of God's image. I wanted them to die an eternal death outside of grace—no mercy. The brutal hardness that would destroy such a tenderhearted woman still infuriates me, but I want the Lord to help me pray through my anger.

I try to envision them as caged men in need of rescue. I pray for them to be freed by grace. Because in truth, it's only the possibility of spiritual transformation—theirs and mine and yours—that's hope for any of us. When the destroyers become healers and the takers become givers and the ones who curse become the ones who bless, then we're living in the arena of grace.

Lord, to those who would steal, kill, destroy,
be the blinding light blazing on the road to Damascus,
the shine that transforms murderers into rescuers.

Come, heal the broken hearts that break others.
Come, restore the souls bent by sin.
Come, lift us into the arena of grace.

But first, still the turbulence in my mind,
wash away the contempt that corrupts my soul,
in your life, defeat death in me.

chapter 9

BLESSING THAT CANCELS CURSE

THE LIVING TREE

O my great High Priest,
Pour down on us streams of needful grace,
Bless us in all our undertakings,
In every thought of our minds,
Every word of our lips,
Every step of our feet,
Every deed of our hands.
For you live to bless,
Die to bless,
Rise to bless,
Ascend to bless,
Take thy throne to bless,
And now you reign to bless.

A PURITAN BLESSING, MODIFIED

All the crosses I've ever seen have been clean. Polished crosses hanging on sterling chains, wooden crosses suspended over baptisteries, carved stone crosses planted in gardens, a filigree metallic cross hung on the wall over a couch in a friend's living room—none of these crosses look horrifying. None of them are blood stained. When the cross becomes an accessory, it's hard to remember that before it was considered beautiful, it was a symbol of terror. But one day, I was confronted with the cross in a way I had never seen it before.

I walked around a white partition in a gallery at the Southeastern Center for Contemporary Art. Sunlight streamed through a wall of glass windows. Across from me hung a luminous photograph of a crucifix—Jesus on the cross. His body and the tree seemed fashioned of one substance; I wasn't sure what it was, but it glowed. Jesus was suspended in light, or enveloped by light—no, actually, it was as if he was composed of light.

The color surrounding the cross grew darker on the fringes of the image until it sank almost to blood red at the edges. To borrow a description from the novelist Willa Cather, the light "was both intense and soft, with a ruddiness as of much-multiplied candlelight, an aura of red in its flames."[1] In the photograph, it seemed the cross itself was the light source and the diffused glow illuminating the image emanated from the man bound to it. The cross and the man were pure shine. Or so it seemed from a distance.

I walked closer. I saw tiny bubbles suspended in the light. Then I glanced at the title—*Piss Christ*, by Andres Serrano.

The beautiful amber glow around the cross was light shining through the artist's own urine.

Let's pause here a moment. Take a breath. If you felt a wave of revulsion, I'm right there with you. But let's try and understand what we're feeling and why we're feeling it, because contemplating this work will take us deeper into the meaning of the cross. And if we want to understand the offense of the Crucifixion for those who witnessed it in person in the first century, then this is a journey we need to take.

Urinating on anything or anyone is an act intended to humiliate. And seeing a symbol and a Savior that we love bathed in filth this way is deeply disturbing. I grew up singing about "the wondrous cross," so it's painful to see it degraded. But the disturbing truth is that everything about the Crucifixion was humiliating.

The nails, the nudity, the brutal exposure, the mocking, the gambling for clothes. The religious leaders who arranged a farce of a trial, the soldiers who pressed a thorny crown onto Jesus' head, the mob who jeered, the thief hanging on a cross nearby who challenged Jesus to "save himself" as he gasped for air. The mockery was intended to shame. If I refuse to acknowledge the humiliation of the Crucifixion, I haven't really seen the cross.

The method behind the making of Serrano's photograph drew fury from those who found his approach blasphemous. When shown at a gallery in Avignon, France, the artwork was attacked by vandals wielding hammers, an act of violence laden with dark irony. Meanwhile, in America, a firestorm of criticism surrounded the artwork after it got the attention of vocal politicians. And although I understand why the piece was deeply offensive to many, I wonder if, in the midst of all the sound and fury, important interpretations of the image were lost. I wonder if all the angry rhetoric surrounding Serrano's photograph might have subsided if those attempting to defend the cross of Christ had realized the artist had given them an opportunity to testify to its meaning.[2] Because Serrano's photograph, in its gut-wrenching insult and ineffable beauty, speaks of the paradox that is the profound mystery of the cross. The cross can take all the offense we can throw at it and still shine.

Standing in the gallery looking at the photograph and blinking back tears, what ultimately struck me was the truth of it: Before the cross was clean, it was filthy. Before the cross was transformed into a symbol of victory, it was a symbol of shame. Before the cross was glory, it was tragedy. Before the cross was a threshold for life, it was an instrument of death. Before the cross became blessing, it was curse. And I feel the burning reality that before it's possible to become blessing, I first have to encounter the curse of the cross and the one who became curse on it.

The Curse of the Tree

He himself bore our sins in his body on the tree.

I PETER 2:24

I've been trained to see the cross as blessing, but that's not what the Jews standing around the cross the day Jesus died saw. That dark day, they could never have perceived the tree as blessing—they would have seen only curse.

Two passages give us insight into this way of seeing the cross—1 Peter 2 and Galatians 3. Let's start with Peter's thoughts and then move to Paul's.

When Peter described the meaning of Jesus' crucifixion, he didn't use the typical Greek word for *cross*. Instead, he used the word for *tree*. Jesus, Peter says, "bore our sins in his body on the *tree*" (1 Peter 2:24, emphasis added).[3] Why that word? I do a little digging and learn that it wasn't the only time Peter used the Greek word for tree, *xulon*, instead of the word for cross. I flip to Peter's sermons in Acts—one to the Jewish religious leaders and another to a Roman soldier named Cornelius and his family. These messages are among some of the earliest reflections on the meaning of the cross by those who had been closest to Jesus. And in both instances, Peter refers to the cross as *a tree*. He says the people killed Jesus "by hanging him on *a tree*" (Acts 5:30, 10:39, emphasis added).

It wasn't necessary for Peter to substitute the word *tree* for *cross*, but Peter's word choice isn't incidental. He's alluding to a law recorded in Deuteronomy 21:22-23, which says that a criminal who is hanged *on a tree* is cursed by God. In his magisterial work *The Cross of Christ*, John Stott contemplates the implications of Peter's word choice:

> The apostles were quite familiar with this legislation,
> and with its implication that Jesus died under
> the divine curse. Yet instead of hushing it up,
> they deliberately drew people's attention to it. So
> evidently they were not embarrassed by it. They did
> not think of Jesus as in any sense deserving to be
> accursed by God. They must, therefore, have at least

begun to understand *that it was our curse which he was bearing.*[4]

Jesus' death "on a tree" should have been incontrovertible evidence that Jesus *wasn't* the Messiah, the one who would rescue and redeem God's people. But Peter's repeated reference to *the tree* on which Jesus died suggests that he was already, in the early days after Jesus' ascension, grappling with the full gravity of what had happened on the cross—that Jesus became the curse in our place, taking the weight of our sin and rebellion on himself.

While Peter nods in the direction of the cross as a symbol of curse, in the book of Galatians, the apostle Paul spells it out explicitly. He quotes directly from the passage in Deuteronomy that Peter only alluded to: "Christ redeemed us from the curse of the law by becoming a curse for us—for it is written, 'Cursed is everyone who is hanged on a tree'" (Galatians 3:13).

From our vantage point in the twenty-first century, the concept of living under the threat of the curse of the law may feel foreign and distant. But for Peter, Paul, and their Jewish contemporaries, the curse of the law was a crisis. In the previous verses, Paul explains, "For all who rely on works of the law are under a curse; for it is written, 'Cursed be everyone who does not abide by all things written in the Book of the Law, and do them'" (Galatians 3:10). The Book of the Law Paul has in mind is the Torah, the law given by God to Moses on Mount Sinai and summed up in the book of Deuteronomy. In order to appreciate the gravity of what the curse meant to Paul and to those living in its shadow, stick with me for a minute as we turn our attention to the book that is framed by a choice—obey and live in God's blessing or disobey and experience the curse.

The Curse of the Law

After a grueling forty years of wandering in the desert, the people of Israel have finally arrived at the border of the Promised Land—this is the setting for the book of Deuteronomy. But before crossing over the Jordan River into their future home, Moses impresses on the people that living in God's blessing is dependent on their obedience to the law. If they keep it, they'll live in God's blessing; but if they break the law, they'll be cursed with exile from the land. To help them visualize these two opposing futures, Moses details a ceremony of blessing and curse to be performed when they arrive in the land. The ceremony will stand as public recognition of the peoples' commitment to God's law and as a way of sealing the promise God is making with Israel into a legally binding relationship called a covenant.

God's law was intended to create a society of people that would be a light to the nations, a people who reflect his good, just, and holy character. Among other things, the people must be fully devoted to the God who had redeemed them from a life of slavery, loving him with their whole heart and soul. They must be upright and honest in their dealings with one another, welcoming foreigners and caring for the vulnerable. If the people abide by the law—honoring it, keeping it, ordering their society according to it—then God promises to bless them. But if the people forget God and live according to their own desires and cravings, then they will experience curse.

We don't expect to find theater in the Bible, but Deuteronomy describes theater scripted by God himself. God directs half the tribes of Israel to stand on Mount Gerizim, the mountain symbolizing blessing, and the other half on Mount Ebal, the mountain symbolizing curse. When the people are in position, the Levites read the obligations of the law aloud; all the people confirm by saying "Amen." No one stands in the valley between because there is no middle ground. There is only a future defined by either blessing or curse. As an extremely sobering prelude to this ceremony, God directs the people to engrave all the details of the law on stones covered in plaster and set them up *on Mount Ebal*—the mountain of curse, not the mountain of blessing (Deuteronomy 27:1-26).

I imagine the tribes standing at attention, the words of the law reverberating across the valley. "I have set before you life and death, blessing and curse. Therefore choose life," Moses urges (Deuteronomy 30:19). The choice seems obvious, doesn't it? Of course we'll take the blessing.

I've listened to preachers who love to sell the beauty of the blessings listed in Deuteronomy: "Blessed shall you be in the city, and blessed shall you be in the field. Blessed shall be the fruit of your womb and the fruit of your ground and the fruit of your cattle . . ." (Deuteronomy 28:3-4). They hold the blessing up to the light, admiring the glint and glimmer of prosperity, health, and security, promising we can appropriate these blessings right now. They dazzle with the blessing, ripping the verses out of context, all the while obscuring the reality that the blessing in Deuteronomy is conditional.

The covenant in Deuteronomy is conditioned on the people's belief *and* behavior. It's conditioned on their willingness to follow this law—*all of it, every minute detail*—together as a community.[5] This covenant, with its promise of blessing and threat of curse, wasn't made with an individual. It was made between God and a particular nation, at a particular place, at a particular time in history. So the problem for any preacher trying to sell this blessing is that if Israel couldn't keep the law and attain the blessing, then neither can we. Prosperity-gospel preachers conveniently mask the reality that the other side of this covenant is curse.

Deuteronomy presents two divergent paths forward and then shows in blinding detail what lies at the end of each of those paths. Preachers don't often dwell on Deuteronomy 27 and 28, but a quick read reveals that the litany of curses for disobedience is much longer than the list of blessings. This imbalance serves both as a warning and a bleak fore-shadowing of the future—curse and exile are on the horizon. Futility, theft, siege, blindness, sickness, starvation, rape, the brutality of mothers eating their own afterbirth, of parents consuming their own children—all the horrors of curse climax in a vision of being stripped and taken in captivity back to Egypt and offered in the slave market where no one wants to buy. This is a portrait of humanity eviscerated. It's a portrait of spiritual and physical exile.

Moses was more than a leader; he was also a prophet. And the conclusion of Deuteronomy is a prophetic word. The people won't keep God's law. They'll disobey, indulge their passions, sell their hearts and their children to other gods. Just as Adam and Eve were exiled from the Garden as a result of their rebellion, the people of Israel will be exiled from the good land.

But then . . .

But then, God himself will return to rescue and restore them. God himself will replace their hearts of stone with hearts of flesh so they can live once more in a state of blessing (Deuteronomy 28:45-47, 30:1-10).

I know this is a spare sketch of a complex book, but it's important to understand the context for the "law" that Paul references in Galatians 3. Because when Paul says that "Christ redeemed us from the curse of the law by becoming a curse for us" (verse 13), the litany of curses climaxing in exile from God's presence is what he's talking about. If we want to understand the curse Jesus bore in his body on the tree, then we have to keep the bone-chilling curses of Deuteronomy in view. To be cursed by God meant to be exiled from the goodness of grace, torn from the shadow of God's protecting wings. It was, ultimately, the condition of being utterly forsaken by God. "My God, my God, why have you forsaken me?" Jesus cried from the cross (Matthew 27:46).[6] This was the cry of exile—it was the culmination of curse.

When God Died

Years ago, I picked my daughter up from school on a brilliant spring day. It was nearly Easter, and it was one of those days when there's not even a whiff of death in the air. Everywhere the austere beauty of winter had given way to the fecundity of spring. Wisteria vines twined their tendrils around iron gates, and fragrant purple blossoms as heavy as ripe grapes hung from balcony rails. Fragile sparks of citron-colored leaves emerged from the branches that just a month ago hid all this riotous life under their leathery bark cloaks. The hum of life was breaking through cracks in the asphalt and the seams of sidewalks in a tangle of grasses, dandelions, and stray daisies. How could I think about Crucifixion on a day like this?

I was walking beside a good friend, and we were trailing our kids, who were just a few steps ahead of us. We could hear them chatting about Easter. There would be chocolate, of course, and candy, and eggs to dip-dye. But what does it all mean? What are we celebrating? My daughter piped up with an answer that knocked the wind out of me like a punch to the gut: "Easter is the holiday when God died," she said.

I kept walking, but inside, I was reeling from the blow. This framing of a holiday I associate with life and the defeat of death sounded so unnerving coming from the lips of a five-year-old. Had my tiny daughter been reading too much Nietzsche? In her naive proclamation, I caught strains of his strident declaration—God is dead.

I leaned over and interjected into the conversation that we also celebrate Jesus' resurrection. But *resurrection* is a big word for a five-year-old, and I could see that her definition of the holiday still struck her as satisfactory.

Kids are so remarkably talented at calling out severe truth that it's possible to obscure with adult explanations. If we say that Jesus is God and affirm that Jesus died on the cross, then it seems perfectly logical to say that God died. Without even knowing what a syllogism is, my daughter made a classic logical leap, without taking into account the nuances of Trinitarian theology. (We were still working on doctrinal basics with her. I mean, she was five.)

In this case, the syllogism doesn't hold. God the Father and the Spirit did not die! Still, her comment touched on the profound mystery at the crux of the cross—the exile of the Son from the presence of the Father, the death of one person of the united, three-person God. "This infinite distance between God and God," reflects Simone Weil, "this supreme tearing apart, this agony beyond all others, this marvel of love, is the crucifixion. Nothing can be further from God than that which has been made accursed."[7]

Jesus, the source of blessing and the author of life, became the curse—the representative of Israel's exile and our alienation from God. Christ didn't just die on the cross; he took the whole weight of the curse of sin and death into his own body. Jesus, Martin Luther explained, didn't just carry the curse on his shoulders—he took it into his being.

> Holy Writ does not say that Christ *was under the curse*. It says directly that Christ *was made a curse*. . . . Although this and similar passages may be properly explained by saying that Christ was made a sacrifice for the curse and for sin, yet in my judgment it is better to leave these passages stand as they read: Christ was made sin itself; *Christ was made the curse itself.*[8]

Eugene Peterson's rendering of Galatians 3:13 in *The Message* brings out this dimension of meaning so beautifully:

"Christ redeemed us from that self-defeating, cursed life by absorbing it completely into himself."

Jesus might have been like us in his humanity, but he was entirely different from us in his divinity. He was *one* with God—essentially unified in spirit and mind. And this truth is what makes the cross so mysterious, so painful, and so wonderful. God the Son suffered exile from God the Father so that our relationship with God could be restored. This is "the mystery of human redemption made possible by the mystery of God's Trinity: The One who was offended bears the burden of the offense."[9] Through the cross, Paul explains, "God was reconciling the world to himself" (2 Corinthians 5:19).

Only by the total identification of Jesus' being with the curse could he break its power over us. Remember Eden— there, the curse was a result of human initiative, a consequence of sin. And from Adam and Eve down through countless generations to us today, each one of us sinned, and so we were all under curse. We "filled [our] lungs with polluted unbelief, and then exhaled disobedience. We all did it, all of us doing what we felt like doing, when we felt like doing it, all of us in the same boat" (Ephesians 2:2-3, MSG).

The curse was ours. But Jesus took the curse that was ours and made it his.

When Peter talked about what happened when Jesus was hung on the tree, he said Jesus *bore* our sins. This verb means "to carry up" or "to endure," and it's the same verb found in Isaiah 53, a passage emphasizing the vicarious suffering of the Servant of God, which facilitates our spiritual healing.

> Surely he has borne *our* griefs
> and carried *our* sorrows . . .
> But he was pierced for *our* transgressions;
> he was crushed for *our* iniquities;
> upon him was the chastisement that brought *us* peace,
> and with his wounds *we* are healed.
>
> ISAIAH 53:4-5, EMPHASIS ADDED

The shift between the singular third-person and the plural first-person pronoun is powerful—Jesus endured the penalty for sins that were not *his*—they were *ours*. Theologians call this idea "substitutionary atonement," a term for the concept that Peter communicates so concisely when, echoing Isaiah, he says that Jesus "*himself* bore *our* sins in *his* body." The wounding of *one individual* precipitated the healing of *you all—plural.* "By his wounds," concludes Peter, "you [*plural*] have been healed" (1 Peter 2:24).[10] This spiritual healing is effective for individuals who repent and believe and for the community of faith as a whole. Peter is describing the possibility of life in restored community liberated from the power of sin and the threat of eternal death, which is no less than a "new life-reality."[11]

Christ bore the humiliation of the curse of the cross so that we could be healed of the sickness of our souls, or in Peter's language, "that we might die to sin and live to righteousness" (1 Peter 2:24). *Righteousness* can mean right conduct before God, but the righteousness Peter has in mind is first and foremost *relational,* involving a return to God. The righteous one dies, Peter says, "that he might bring us to God" (1 Peter 3:18).

Return to Live in God's Blessing

One brisk August day, I stepped off a ferry onto an island constructed of some of the oldest granite on earth. I was wrapped in a wool sweater and scarf, a raincoat tied around my waist. The islands of the Scottish Hebrides are so far north that even at the height of summer, the breeze off the sea is bracing. But it's not the cold that struck me—it was the extraordinary quality of the light.

The play of the sun on the surface of the sea electrified the water, so it looked like living light, a shimmering mirror reflecting the pure cerulean sky. When I turned my gaze to the landscape, I still sensed this dance of light across the hedges, through the grasses, and over the gentle pastures, flecked all through with granite knobs. There was a strange dissonance between the stillness of this old land where sheep grazed in lazy nonchalance, the stalwartness of the ancient rock, and the vibrant quality of this flood of light. I was fortunate to have visited on a sunny day. I suspect the overall effect is somewhat different on the frigid, overcast days of winter.

I was, like so many pilgrims before me, visiting Iona, a tiny island only a mile wide and three and a half miles long. Over long centuries, this small stamp of land has been shrouded with holiness. It was said that there is a rainbow bridge connecting heaven and earth. The day I visited, I didn't see any rainbows, but I did see a bridge that binds our earthly reality with a heavenly inheritance.

I saw a monumental carved stone cross, weathered but still teeming with life. Its beams held images of stories from the Bible laced together with intertwining living vines. The cross stood outside the chapel dedicated to Saint Columba, an Irish missionary who landed on the island along with twelve companions in AD 563, with the aim of evangelizing the pagan Picts of Scotland. Their mission ultimately transformed the religious landscape of Northern Europe. Now only three monumental stone crosses are left standing on the island, but it's thought that during the medieval period, there might have been as many as one thousand—every square inch of land testifying to the blessing of Christ.

The anonymous masters who carved the imagery into the stone worked under the assumption that the stories of Scripture anticipate the event of the cross and are completed by it. Looking down at the base of Saint Matthew's Cross, I saw two figures separated by the trunk of a fruit-laden tree—Adam and Eve in the Garden.[12] Roughly fifteen hundred years ago, the artists on Iona understood that the event that unfolded around the tree in Eden precipitated the need for another tree—the cross.

I stretched out on the grass not far from the base of Saint Matthew's Cross, feeling the earth firm under my back. The contours of the image of Adam and Eve separated from one another by the trunk of a tree were still fresh in my mind. I closed my eyes, but in the intensity of the daylight, all I saw was a veil of amber red, the same color that bathed Andres Serrano's photograph of Jesus on the cross. And these images began to merge in my mind, because there is an inescapable connection between the tree in Eden and the tree on Golgotha. One tree ushered in curse, the other blessing. One tree drove a wedge between God and humanity, the other offers reconciliation. One tree provoked rebellion, the other is our peace.

I can hear the words of the blessing of Numbers 6 reverberating in my mind. The blessing that anticipates experiencing God's shining face ultimately culminates in the blessing of peace: "May the LORD look on you with favor and *give you peace.*" The blessing of peace takes on the full depth of its meaning in the shadow of the cross because it was on this tree that God reconciled the world to himself, "*making peace* by the blood of his cross" (Colossians 1:20, emphasis added). If there's any sentimentality still clinging to the concept of blessing, the cross utterly strips it away, exposing the reality that blessing is most fully expressed in the sacrificial giving of self for the sake of others.

To experience the healing the cross offers, I have to fully identify with the one who hung from it. And so, lying flat on the ground with the cross over my shoulder, I recalled Paul's testimony in Galatians: "I have been crucified with Christ. It is no longer I who live, but Christ who lives in me. And the life I now live in the flesh I live by faith in the Son of God, who loved me and *gave himself for me*" (Galatians 2:20, emphasis added). Christ gave himself—his givenness is the ground of blessing. The practice of blessing begins here, at the foot of this living tree. It starts by receiving the one who gave himself on it.

On the tree, Jesus canceled the curse of Eden and the curse of the law in Deuteronomy so that we could enter into the blessing of Christ through faith—a new covenant written on hearts, not on stones. The blessing of the cross isn't a possession; it's a relationship with the one who blesses. The practice of blessing isn't a finite act or object; it's an ongoing way of relating that involves the whole self. Being called to bless means to live given. And if I've truly experienced the blessing of the cross, then the givenness that I see in Christ should characterize my life too.

Lying between earth and heaven on the windswept island that smelled of the salty sea, feeling the dirt under my fingers and the sun on my face, I rested in the presence of the bridge connecting heaven and earth—the cross. The richness of the concept of spiritual blessing encompassing both salvation and the maturing and thriving of the entire community of faith is the *eulogia Christou*, or the "blessing of Christ" (Romans 15:29).[13] And the way into that blessing is through the one who took his last breath on the tree. Jesus, keep me near your cross: the one that subverts violence and puts an end to death, the one that is our salvation, that holds out hope of restoration, the cross that is the ultimate expression of blessing, the way to return to you.

May you see the light playing over the surface of the waters,
witness the movement of the river
flowing through wandering exiles
generation to generation until
like a flood
it runs through the body of a bruised Savior.

May the rush of living water call you to return
to be healed
to be free
to be given.

chapter 10

TRANSFORMATION

WRESTLING FOR BLESSING

I will make with them a covenant of peace and
banish wild beasts from the land,
so that they may dwell securely
in the wilderness and sleep in the woods.
And I will make them and the places all around my hill a blessing,
and I will send down the showers in their season;
they shall be showers of blessing.

EZEKIEL 34:25-26

"Live water heals memories"—that's a line from Annie Dillard. And of all people, she should know. She spent a year hanging out by Tinker Creek, reflecting on the savage complexity and outrageous beauty of the life that thrived in and along streams of living water. "So many things have been shown to me on these banks," she marvels, "so much light has illumined me by reflection here where the water comes down, that I can hardly believe that this grace never flags, that the pouring from ever-renewable sources is endless, impartial, free."[1]

Ever-renewable, endless, impartial, free—she might as well be talking about God's blessing. All those attributes apply to the blessing that flows through the pages of Scripture, originating with God's first words to Adam and Eve in Eden, meandering through the family of Abraham, rushing through the prophetic visions of Ezekiel, Isaiah, and Jeremiah. In one of the most immersive visions in the Old Testament, Ezekiel finds himself on the banks of a river. He sees living water bubbling up from under the altar within the temple of God. A stream of water trickles out of the southern gate and flows toward the east. He slips off his sandals and dips his toes in the water. He wades into the river that begins ankle-deep and gradually widens and deepens until finally, it becomes a river deep enough to swim in, "a river that could not be passed through" (Ezekiel 47:1-12).

The Lord asks him, "Have you seen this?" Do you perceive what all this means? Here's the river that transforms salty dead places into lush gardens. Here's the river that gives life to anyone caught up in its current. Here's the river that nourishes the roots of all kinds of trees that "will bear fresh fruit every month, because the water for them flows from the sanctuary. Their fruit will be for food, and their leaves for healing" (Ezekiel 47:12). Here's the living water that satisfies thirsty souls. Here's the river that symbolizes the coming of the era of the blessing of the Lord. Here's the river that's "symbolic of the life-giving presence of God."[2] "And behold," exclaims Ezekiel, "the glory of the God of Israel was coming from the east. And the sound of his coming was *like the sound of many waters*" (Ezekiel 43:2, emphasis added).

Ezekiel's alluvial vision gleams with a brilliant eschatological hope—a new heavens and a new earth suffused by the eternal shine of God, where those "blessed" by the Lord will live and reign forever and ever. This is the future foreseen by John in the last chapters of Revelation, where his apocalyptic imagery culminates in the picture of a river "bright as crystal" flowing from God's throne. This river nourishes the roots of the tree of life that bears fruit year-round and, John reveals, "the leaves of the tree were for the healing of the nations" (Revelation 22:1-3).

We'll return to the banks of this river soon, but right now, I have another river in view. Before we can bathe in the dawn, we must wrestle through a long, dark night.

Wrestling in the Dark

Sometime after the loss of Eden and before Ezekiel's electrifying visions, Jacob, the grandson of Abraham, finds himself lingering by the edge of a stream around nightfall. It's said the sound of moving water calms the soul. And I have a hunch that's why Jacob wants to sleep by the brook of Jabbok the night before meeting his brother, Esau, for the first time in twenty long years.

Anxiety must have been eating away at Jacob's heart. As he sits listening to the sound of the water eddying around smooth stones, perhaps he is replaying scenes from the theft of a blessing that left his brother raging. Perhaps he is praying that living water will heal this painful memory and cleanse his soiled character. After all, from birth, Jacob's name—*the deceiver*—has more or less defined his identity. He's been a thief, taking rather than receiving. The impulse to grasp what hadn't been given that was at work in Adam and Eve is there in Jacob, too. After the taking, he hasn't been home since.

But now Jacob is poised to return. He hesitates at the border, lingering at the river that runs through his present like a question mark, asking if his past will determine his future. He crouches in the dark at the margins of home, doubting there can be a return. His longing for forgiveness rises as the sun sets. And after all these years, he's still desperate for one thing—a blessing.

This is the strangest aspect of a very strange story. Why would Jacob need a blessing? Jacob has already been blessed in nearly every imaginable way. At this point in his life, he's the guy who has everything. He's the possessor of his father's inheritance, *bekorah*, and his father's spoken blessing, *berakah*. He has two wives and eleven sons, and he shepherded Laban's flocks so skillfully that his uncle was reluctant to let him go, confessing that "the LORD has blessed me *because of you*" (Genesis 30:27, emphasis added). He's become fabulously rich, the master of flocks of sheep and herds of camels. There is nothing material he needs. But wealth isn't the sort of blessing he's craving.

The well-being Jacob is seeking is spiritual, relational. He needs God's blessing of *shalom*—of forgiveness, of reconciliation, of healed relationships, of peace within his family. When we first met Jacob in Genesis, he was a grasping opportunist: manipulative, greedy, scheming, open to using any means to acquire a blessing, including deceiving *his own father*. But the man whose character was so soiled it appeared unredeemable experiences an extraordinary transformation. The turning point for Jacob is here at the brook of Jabbok, during a wrestling match with a mysterious assailant.

Events that unfold in the dark are often disorienting. And there is a disorienting quality to Jacob's encounter on the banks of the brook. Jacob never knows the identity of his combatant; he only knows he struggles with someone strong. An angel, a messenger, a mediator for God's presence—he wrestles with the guy all night. He tightens his grip and holds on despite exhaustion from the prolonged tension. As the sky starts to lighten, he finally confesses his deepest desire: "I will not let you go *unless you bless me*" (Genesis 32:26, emphasis added).

I feel like I'm right beside Jacob. I'm wrestling for a blessing too. I try desperately to hold on to invisible divine presence while longing to live in the blessing of peace realized in flourishing relationships. And in this longing, I'm not so far from Eve glancing back at Eden as she stumbled out of the Garden she forfeited to satisfy her own desire. I'm not so far from Abraham gazing up at the stars and glancing sideways at a barren wife, wondering when, if ever, God's promised blessing would fall on him. I'm right there with Sarah, laughing bitterly out of the barrenness of a soul tired of waiting for God's promises to be fulfilled.

Blessing Inspires Transformation

For weeks, I've been flipping between Genesis 27, Jacob's stealing of the blessing, and Genesis 48 and 49, Jacob's blessing of his grandchildren and children before his death. At the end of his life, Jacob is a different man—the deceiver has become wise, discerning, patient. To understand how Jacob matured from a taker into a giver, I search the intervening years. And there, in the in-between spaces, I find the key: three encounters with God, each marked by a blessing.

First, God met and blessed Jacob at Bethel, while he was on the run, fleeing from Esau. Then God encountered Jacob at the brook of Jabbok just before he reunited with his brother. And finally, God met him again at Bethel, just before the death of his wife Rachel and his father, Isaac (Genesis 28, 32, 35). In each instance, God's blessing coincided with a momentous transition in Jacob's life. God met him as he was on the move—on the way from one reality to another—and promised to be with him (Genesis 28:15).

The refining of Jacob's character didn't happen overnight, and it wasn't the result of a single encounter with God. Jacob matured through a series of encounters—*through a series of blessings*—that worked on him over the span of his life. It was the blessing of God's enduring presence that ultimately transformed his character.

When God first approached Jacob at Bethel, it wasn't when

he was chasing after blessing; it was when he was sound asleep, unguarded and vulnerable. On the way to Harran, exhausted from the journey, Jacob stretched out on the ground with a rock propped under his head as a pillow. There, in the middle of nowhere, he surrendered to a dream flooded with spiritual vision. He saw a ladder connecting heaven and earth, angels ascending and descending. In this place where spiritual and physical reality mingled, Jacob met the Lord (Genesis 28:10-22).

After Jacob's dishonest dealings with his father, I expect God to chasten him. I expect God to say: "I'd really like to bless you, but only on the condition that you behave yourself and stop lying and cheating and taking . . ." But God doesn't say any of those things. His revelation is brimming with blessing, not condemnation.

God's first statement to Jacob is an affirmation, "*I am* the LORD." The explicit focus is on God, not on Jacob. The given blessing is dependent on God's character, not on Jacob's moral perfection. Blessing flows from God's goodness and purpose to bless all the families of the earth, not in response to Jacob's worthiness.

The blessing once given to Abraham is now explicitly given to him together with a promise of God's abiding presence: "In you and your offspring shall all the families of the earth be blessed. Behold, I am with you and will keep you wherever you go" (Genesis 28:14-15). Even though the blessing is not dependent on Jacob, it begins working inside him, reorienting his heart, reordering his affections. Jacob cannot possibly misunderstand that this blessing is directed to him and is for him. He's left to decide if he will walk with the Lord and live in the blessing.

At Bethel, God's work inside Jacob has begun, but it is far from done. In Jacob's response to the revelation, there is still a subtle bargaining at work in his words: "*If* God will be with me and will keep me in this way that I go," he says, "*then* the LORD shall be my God" (Genesis 28:20-21, emphasis added). *If . . . then*: Jacob's devotion is conditional. He still has terms. He will only extend trust if the Lord makes good on his promise. But by the time he returns to meet his brother Esau, he's no longer bargaining. Before Jacob can make peace with Esau, he must find lasting peace with God.

A Prayer by the Water

It's Friday night, less than a week after New Year's. I just dropped my daughter off at her ballet class, and I have more than an hour to kill. I sense a pull to walk by the water. So I set off downhill in a hurry because I'm hoping to catch the sunset. In Istanbul, we may not have a stream, but we have a strait—the Bosporus Strait. It's the thread of deep, fast-moving water that connects the Black Sea to the Sea of Marmara. The currents are so strong, they can carry tanker ships off course. Only specially trained captains are allowed to navigate the treacherous passage.

I walk downhill at a clip, passing bars, boutiques, bakeries, shops selling comic books and vintage vinyl albums. The lights are on in a gallery owned by an acquaintance who lives in the first apartment we rented in the city, but I don't stop to pause and chat. I skirt the streets leading to a crowded, narrow alley lined with fish sellers, cafés, and pastry shops displaying fresh baklava sprinkled with ground pistachio.

I dodge traffic at an intersection leading to the harbor. As I step up onto the curb, a girl with long wavy brown hair pulls me aside and asks for directions. She's not far from where she's headed, so I gesture in the direction she needs to go. As she takes off, it occurs to me that maybe I don't look as foreign as I feel.

I glance up and see a few wispy pink clouds dissolving into the darkening sky and I'm afraid I may have missed the show, so I pick up my pace. I rush through a haze of smoke billowing from the cart where chestnuts are roasting and fly past the man hawking *midye*, fresh mussels. (In all my years in the city, I've never once been tempted by the mussels.) I keep the docks for the commuter ferries to my right while rounding the corner past the parking lot on my left, and now, in this wide-open space where the jetty frames the harbor, I can breathe. I face the sea. Although the sun is gone, a streak of fuchsia still lights up the horizon.

I know this view so well. Across the water, the silhouette of the old, walled city that was once called Constantinople is crowned by Sultanahmet, Hagia Sophia, and Topkapi Palace, all plum in the twilight. Seagulls cry, circling over my shoulder. The lights of container ships blink on the horizon. It's a still evening, almost no breeze, so the waves lap gently at the foot of the massive granite stones that make up the sea wall where my kids love throwing chunks of stone into the water.

I turn to walk along the path where my daughter first rode a bike on the afternoon of her fifth birthday. I can still picture her, pedaling tentatively while teetering between the training wheels, the sun bleaching her hair. It occurs to me that I've lived in this city longer than any other place I've lived in my life. But is it home? A family clambers up onto the sea wall to take a picture in the fading light. A little girl who must be about the age of my son cries out, *"Baba, beni tut!"*—Dad, hold me!

Her petition rises in me like a prayer. In a way, this is what I've been praying for years: *Father, hold me.* I've needed to be held through the days when I sat here contemplating the movement of the water and lamenting the reality that I'm raising a family in rented spaces, where my suitcases are always stacked on the shelves in my closet over my hanging clothes, an ever-present reminder of transience. The pages of my passport are covered with entry and exit stamps, a record of all the miles I've logged in the air, suspended over the places other people put down roots and make home. *Father, hold me, because the only home I have to hold on to is you.*

Like Jacob, I'm wrestling to hold on to God while begging him to keep holding on to me. The night before Jacob wrestles with the angel at the brook of Jabbok, he meets God in a desperate prayer—the only extended prayer in the book of Genesis. This sincere prayer is so different from his first prayer at Bethel, revealing just how far he's come. There are no more conditions because he's no longer bargaining—he's confessing. Jacob acknowledges what God has known all along, admitting, *"I am not worthy* of the least of all the deeds of steadfast love and all the faithfulness that you have shown to your servant" (Genesis 32:10, emphasis added).

In Jacob's prayer, there is no pretense, no dissembling, no boast. Jacob confronts his greatest fears by putting them into words, and he lays them at the Lord's feet. He has come to terms with two things: his unworthiness and his utter dependence on God's steadfast love. In confession, he places his entire being in God's hands. He's learned that he cannot manipulate God into extending blessing. He can only cry out transparently, desperately, honestly.

God doesn't answer Jacob's prayer immediately. The suspense builds. Will the relational and spiritual conflict have a peaceful resolution? Or will Jacob's heart forever be plagued by the curse of fear?

Jacob's internal struggle is so intense it's given visual expression in the wrestling match by the brook of Jabbok—a physical struggle that reflects the war within Jacob's soul. He needs to be reconciled with God before he can be reconciled with his estranged brother. As dawn breaks amber on the horizon, Jacob still clings to his combatant. Even after his hip is wrenched out of socket by a glancing touch, he refuses to let go, stating insistently, "I will not let you go *unless you bless me*" (Genesis 32:26, emphasis added).

God honors Jacob's tenacity by giving him a new name—*Israel*—a name that means one who strives with God (Genesis 32:28). Jacob has been transformed: He is no longer the deceiver; he is the one who has wrestled with God for a blessing and prevailed. Jacob limps away rewarded with a blessing because even in his weakness, he kept holding on.

The one who strives with God—this name becomes the name of those God chooses as his own. He blesses the ones who wrestle. He calls the doubters, the deceivers, the 212 takers, the bargainers. He chooses the flawed vessels, the weak ones, the weasels, the prodigals. He calls out to the ones up at midnight, wracked by anxiety and angst. He whispers to those doubting in the dark. God welcomes the ones who hang on to him for dear life, refusing to let go. But he doesn't leave them the way he finds them, because his blessing transforms character and instills faith. This transformation is often painful—in Jacob's case, it wrenched his hip out of joint, leaving him with a limp. But the struggle is worth the wound because through it, he meets the source of blessing.

Jacob calls the place by the brook where he wrestled all night *Peniel*, a name that means "face of God." He exclaims with genuine awe, "I have *seen* God face to face, and yet my life has been delivered." As Jacob speaks these words, he is bathed in light. Literally. The text actually says that "the sun rose upon him" (Genesis 32:30-31, emphasis added). "This scenic depiction portrays Jacob's spiritual landscape."[3] His soul has been illuminated. He has *seen* God; he has been face-to-face with divine presence. Now he's a man who truly sees.

Come to the Waters

It's nearly night by the banks of the Bosporus. The deep smoky violet of the sky is reflected in the sea. The horizon line nearly vanishes, so the distance between the heavens and the waters covering the earth seems to have disappeared. It'll be hours before the sun rises.

Jacob's fleeting experience of seeing God and being blessed through the seeing was a glimpse of an eternal hope that has not yet dawned. In the last chapters of Revelation, John helps us imagine the era of blessing that awaits us when we finally see the face of God:

> He showed me a river of the water of life, clear as
> crystal, coming from the throne of God and of the
> Lamb, in the middle of its street. On either side of
> the river was the tree of life, bearing twelve kinds of
> fruit, yielding its fruit every month; and the leaves
> of the tree were for the healing of the nations.
> *There will no longer be any curse*; and the throne of
> God and of the Lamb will be in it, and His bond-
> servants will serve Him; they will see His face, and
> His name will be on their foreheads. And there
> will no longer be any night; and they will not have
> need of the light of a lamp nor the light of the sun,
> because the Lord God will illumine them; and they
> will reign forever and ever.
>
> REVELATION 22:1-5, NASB, EMPHASIS ADDED

This dawn. This illumination. This river cascading with living water. These leaves that heal the nations. *The end of curse forever*. This is an existence that is Eden and the tip-top of Sinai and the glory of the Mount of Transfiguration. But unlike those previous experiences that were fleeting moments, this existence endures. This is a vision of eternity.

But we're not there yet. We live suspended between a blessing already realized in Christ and a state of blessing anticipated but not yet fulfilled. The current of history streams toward an ocean whose depths we cannot fathom. Our lives occupy the space between the blessing of the cross and the surpassing goodness of an everlasting era of blessing when a renewed heaven and earth will be knit together as one (Revelation 21–22). Even as I long to live in a world where there is no longer any lingering curse, I realize that the practice of blessing is a way of leaning into that future reality right now.

So in this between time, I cling to God like Jacob, buoyed by the reminder that God's blessing has always flowed through imperfect people.

Sarah, a barren woman whose faith was stretched thin by her impatience with God.

Isaac, a parent whose lack of vision hampered his ability to bless his children well.

Jacob, a deceiver whose manipulation strained his relationships.

The disciples, who were preoccupied with scarcity when they were in the company of the one whose blessing creates abundance.

I can identify with all these characters. Despite their individual weaknesses and sinful impulses, each of them carried God's blessing into the world. In fact, it was precisely their need—barrenness, desperation, and incapacity—that highlighted the beautiful truth that blessing originates with God even when it moves through us. When God's goodness and power overcome our weaknesses for the sake of others, then God receives the glory. If his power transformed their frailties into an opportunity for blessing, then it can transform us, too.

Beginning with God's pivotal call to Abraham to become a river of blessing to all the families of the earth, there has been an expectation that the family God has blessed will become a blessing to others. Through Christ, we're incorporated into that family—the church, a family united by faith and filled with the Spirit (Galatians 3:13-14). This family is a priesthood of believers called to mediate God's blessing to the world. The charge first given to the family of Abraham is a glimpse of the gospel beforehand, and it foreshadows the commissioning of Jesus' followers to go out into the world with a blessing of peace—the blessing of the cross. Jesus intensifies the call to bless in the most challenging way imaginable by inviting us to join him in a ministry of blessing that transcends the natural boundary between friend and enemy, asking us to bless those who curse and do good to those who hate. This countercultural way of relating distinguishes those who stand in the arena of grace. Those who align themselves with Jesus' call reflect the character of God, who is merciful even to those who were once his enemies. And Jesus promises that those who suffer because of their obedience to this hard call are blessed with God's abiding presence now and—with the promise of a future inheritance—a home in the new heavens and earth.

Understanding how blessing is threaded all through the arc of the biblical narrative enables us to see that our lives take on fuller meaning and purpose when they're integrated into this story. I can't possibly bless *all* the families of the earth. But I am perfectly positioned to bless the family God has given me. The practice of blessing starts at home. As I've tried to learn to bless those the Lord has brought near—my husband, my kids, my friends, and my neighbors—I'm beginning to sense that cultivating a lifestyle of blessing has ripple effects beyond the walls of our home. The internal orientation of self that we nurture in our devotional and private lives is the one we carry with us into public spaces as we follow Christ wherever he leads. Christian presence in society should be associated with an ethos characterized by blessing. If our voice in the public sphere is more often tinged with attitudes that convey curse, then we've got to wonder if we've forgotten the dimension of blessing within the biblical story that could give form to our incarnational witness.

Through the lives of people like Francis of Assisi, Saint Columba, Amy Carmichael, and Polycarp, I've been reminded that the practice of blessing has found expression in the life of the church through the centuries. Their obedience to the call to bless might have had varied application, but they all embodied the goodness of God's presence in their own time, blessing through intercession, witness, and action. The orientation of their lives aligned with the current of God's grace. The convictions they espoused were given shape through their way of relating to others that reflected the way God first related to us—through blessing.

This journey to understand the meaning and practice of blessing might have begun as a project to add a few Christian blessings to my conversation, but now I realize that blessing is a pilgrimage into learning how to love. I've seen how God's blessing is a creative force that sustains life and invites us into relationship. His blessing calls us to let go and follow him into uncharted territory. It enables us to see with spiritual vision, transforms us, shapes our identity, and ushers in a climate of flourishing that anticipates the new creation of the world to come. I've learned that a total orientation of the self—attitude, actions, and spoken prayers toward the future good of others—is what's involved in *becoming blessing.* And a distinctly Christian view of blessing acknowledges that God alone is the source of good, that his presence among us is ultimate blessing, and that Jesus' sacrifice on the cross freed us from the curse to find peace with God so that we can live in—and as—blessing.

Paul unpacks the wonder of the blessing we have in Christ in the opening of his letter to the Ephesians, marveling that God has blessed us "with *every spiritual blessing* in the heavenly places." Redemption, justification, being made right in our relationship with God, an experience of the riches of his grace, forgiveness of sin, spiritual insight, revelation of the mystery of his will, and being filled with the Holy Spirit (Ephesians 1:3-14, emphasis added)—these blessings all flow out of receiving the blessing of the cross. And, significantly, it is precisely these spiritual blessings that are the source of the strength and inspiration required to bless sacrificially, giving of ourselves for the good of others. In the moments we live given, we anticipate a future reality in which there will no longer be any curse, only blessing. As we pray for God's goodness to flow through us, we swim with the current toward a vision of a future life along the banks of a river clear as crystal.

Come, come to these waters, sings the prophet Isaiah. Watch and see swords beaten into garden tools, lions lying down with lambs, predators transformed into protectors. Look, says Malachi, and see the sun of righteousness rising with healing in his wings. Wipe away your tears, encourages Jeremiah, and "be radiant over the goodness of the LORD" because your life "shall be like a watered garden." Come, encourages John, let anyone who is thirsty drink deep; let anyone who desires take this water of life without paying a dime. Slip off your sneakers, invites Ezekiel, who's standing in the middle of the river while water soaks the coarse wool of his tunic. Have you seen this? Have you really seen? There's life wherever this water goes.[4]

Breathe In, Breathe Out

I was up all night listening to my daughter breathe. She coughed, her throat constricted, her breathing raspy. I know this sound too well—a distressed seal barking. She had the croup again.

I lifted her out of her bed and brought her into my room. She curled up in my lap as I sat in the rocking chair by the open bedroom window. The cool night air always seems to calm her and ease her labored breathing.

Inhale, exhale, repeat. Holding her, I was reminded how much I need to breathe.

God's blessing is like the oxygen surrounding us—the essential thing we need each moment of each day to keep our souls pumping. It's so strange that some people confuse God's essential blessing with prosperity. Wealth, compared to presence, is a wisp of a shadow, a drop of water as opposed to a running river. God's blessing is something to bathe in, not something to possess, to display. God's blessing is a cosmos, a calling, a cross, a reason for being, a way of relating.

Inhale, exhale, breathe in, breathe out. A life-giving rhythm. We don't just breathe blessing in and hold our breath. Breathing requires an exhale, a release, the slow steady rhythm of drawing in and then letting go.

Inhale, exhale, repeat.

Why are there still so many days that I forget—or refuse— to breathe out? Why are there still so many days that I feel I'm suffocating, holding on to the blessing that would be renewed if I only exhaled? Why do my thoughts still often tend toward negativity and curse, suspecting the motives of those who have wounded me when I should be desiring their good, praying blessing?

I breathe in the dawn, and I exhale, breathing out the praise. *Bless the Lord, O my soul, bless his holy name*—these words are becoming a refrain humming through my days. But this orientation of self must be renewed each and every day, or I find myself sliding back into the natural human pattern of withholding blessing from those who withhold it from me. That's not the pattern I want to define my relationships; it's not the way of life Jesus calls me into. The arena of grace: that's the space where I'll find life. It's the locus of true blessing.

I think of Abraham, that nomad called to be a blessing to all the families of the earth. I think of that father of a multitude of nations with the barren wife who only bore him one miracle son. I think of that traveler always one step away from true home, longing for a homeland. If the pilgrim of faith, even after pitching his tent in the Promised Land, never really felt he had arrived, why would I hope to put down roots in this world?

"You make [us] most blessed forever;" sings the psalmist, "you make [us] glad with the joy of your presence" (Psalm

21:6). And right here I find the heart of blessing. This is where I'll put down roots. This is where I'll find my dwelling place: in God's presence. And I realize that in this life I was never called to arrive. I'm called to become.

> May the grace of the Lord Jesus Christ,
> the steadfast love of the Father,
> and the fellowship of the Spirit
> be with you all.
>
> 2 CORINTHIANS 13:14, AUTHOR'S PARAPHRASE

acknowledgments

The sweet potatoes are in the oven. A little later, I'll be rolling out crust for a chocolate raspberry pie. It's Thanksgiving Day. Despite my promise to myself not to crack open my laptop on a holiday, it occurred to me that there could be no more suitable time to remember and acknowledge all the people who have been part of this journey with me.

I started writing the first chapter of this book four years ago on New Year's Day while sitting at a kitchen table in North Carolina. That autumn, I had walked through a study I had developed on blessing in the Bible with a group of women at First Baptist Church in Hendersonville, North Carolina. Their enthusiasm for the insights that emerged over the weeks we spent together and their confidence that the material should become a book prompted me to begin gathering my notes and outlines into prose. I'm so thankful to them for being sure (more sure than I was myself) that the conversations we'd had should be amplified. They gently nudged me to begin writing.

Although the writing started four years ago, reading and

studying, mulling over certain perplexing Scripture passages, underlining and note-taking spanned roughly a decade. As Turkish friends opened their homes and their culture to me, patiently suffering through my feeble attempts to speak their beautiful language, I began to appreciate the blessings that were incorporated into everyday conversations and to wonder why, as a Christian, I knew so few. For all the afternoons spent sipping *çay* from tulip-shaped glasses, for teaching me to learn to savor *börek* in its countless delicious variations, for generosity and hospitality, Asli, Aysel, Yonca, and Ege, thank you for helping me find home away from home. And to my friend Claire, who piqued my interest in the meaning of Byzantine art and architecture, you are the humblest genius I know, utterly unaware of the brilliance that is so self-evident to anyone who has the joy of knowing you well. Your vibrant curiosity inspires my own, and you cannot fathom how deeply your appreciation for beauty, art, and literature has touched my soul.

What would we do without friends who speak the truth in love? Laura, Beth, Laurel, Priscila, Karla, and Leah, thank you for encouraging and challenging me as I was writing. You often commented on chapters in a way that was refining. Thank you for being part of a community of sisters and friends that keeps me rooted and grounded in love.

One of the difficulties of researching and writing this book from my perch in Istanbul was distance from a good theological library. Without access to pastor Turgay Üçal's books, I would have spent a fortune in international shipping. Thank you so much for sharing the church's library with me and for your deep appreciation for the historical and cultural roots of Christianity. And thank you for welcoming us into fellowship—our faith and practice is richer for the years we spent worshiping with the church in Moda.

Thank you, too, to the fine doctors who were teaching at Regent College in Vancouver, British Columbia, the year we studied on campus. Brilliant lectures elicited many thoughts that eventually made their way into the manuscript. Rikk Watts's passionate apology for the importance of the use of the Old Testament in the New, Maxine Hancock's magnificent reading list for her Jesus in Literature course, and an independent study in Byzantine art and theology with Hans Boersma were all life-giving and thought-provoking. Thank you, in particular, to Iain Provan, who read and commented on an early, meandering draft of these chapters. And thank you to John Stackhouse, who first suggested that if I was really interested in understanding blessing, I should carve out some time to become acquainted with Claus Westermann. I'm so grateful that you prompted me to resume work on the book manuscript after I had laid it aside for months, thinking nothing would come of it.

Although composition tends to be a solitary endeavor, publishing requires a network of relationships. Thank you to Lukas Naugle for passing my book proposal along to people who could bring it to life. The miracle of mobile technology made it possible for me to "sign" the book contract while I was camping out by a lake near Iznik, the site of the ancient city of Nicaea. Thank you to Erik Wolgemuth, who has sharpened the concept of agent for me from one who represents to one who supplies good counsel. It was so reassuring to have a sounding board through the long publishing process.

I'm so grateful to the entire team at NavPress for their creative vision. Thank you, especially, to Don Pape for embracing this project and for being the sort of person who assures a new (and nervous) writer that she is being prayed for. Your intercession was a profound blessing. And thank you to David Zimmerman, whose wit and wisdom made the refining aspect of the editorial process a joy. I was delighted by the original painting made by Dean Renninger for the cover. Thank you for pairing a beautiful image with these words of mine.

No two people have been more concerned about my spiritual formation over the years than my parents, Paula and Ken Hemphill. The abiding love I have for Scripture grew directly from the marvel of hearing my dad teach from it every Sunday up until the time I left home for college. I don't pretend to be an unbiased observer, but I still think he's the best exegetical preacher alive. Mom and Dad, you cultivated respect for God's Word, you helped me trust its veracity, love its language and syntax, appreciate the multiplicity of voices that harmonize so beautifully as they tell one story that holds together from start to finish, Genesis to Revelation—the story that makes us who we are. Thank you for inviting me into that story.

Most of the research and reading for this book happened in the fringe hours—either very early morning or late at night. But despite my best attempts to write when it wouldn't impact my ability to care for my kids, the work often bled into family time. An unfortunate side effect of immersing yourself in a topic is that it isn't always possible to turn off the conceptual flow to attend to important daily interruptions that are an inevitable part of family life. I fear there were a lot of days when Lois, Micah, and Naomi found me gazing into the distance lost in thought rather than engaging in conversation at the dinner table, helping with homework, or asking about their day when they dropped their bookbags by the door. I'm so thankful for your patience with my distraction, your unconditional love, and your collective sense of humor that called me back into the present moments I was missing. You are the joy of my heart.

If there was one person who sacrificed the most for this book to become a reality, it was my husband, Brett. We don't have a dedicated office, so our main dining table was piled with books and notes for months. Thank you so much for giving me the freedom to read, think, and develop these ideas and wrestle with the words that didn't always come together. Thank you for forgiving me when I left the oven on high for hours or let the pasta boil over because I fled the kitchen to go polish a paragraph. By grace and with your help, I managed not to burn the house down. In spite of my tendency to lose myself in words on a page, thank you for making home with me and for being home for me. You are the love of my heart.

Above all, I want to thank the people who are living lives given to God and poured out for the sake of others. I've met some of you in Soviet-era apartments with peeling wallpaper and shoddy plumbing, others in valleys where women still walk to draw water from filthy streams for cooking and cleaning. I've listened to your stories while sorting tiny stones out of rice before dinner or while waiting for the metro during rush hour. You manage to find grace and glory in unexpected places and you persevere, willing to share in the sufferings of Christ because you've tasted the surpassing goodness of knowing God. May the Lord establish the work of your hands and may it endure, multiply, and continue to bear fruit long after you find yourselves strolling along the banks of a river clear as crystal.

May we lean together toward the day when the wolf and lamb will graze side by side, the lion will feast on straw like the ox, and they will not hurt or destroy anywhere on the holy mountain. May it be.

reading and reflection guide

Exploring blessing in the Bible is only fruitful to the extent that we put what we learn into practice. This guide is designed with a fourfold purpose: first, to help you dive deeper into blessing by exploring the context of the Scripture shared in the book; second, to help you reflect on the meaning of these passages and consider how they might apply to your life; third, to help you become familiar with some explicit blessings in the Bible; and finally, to compose and share blessings of your own.

- *Read.* Key Scripture passages provide context for the stories and ideas discussed in the book.

- *Reflect.* Questions prompt personal reflections and help facilitate discussion with a small group.

- *Biblical Blessings.* The practice of blessing isn't about reciting a script; it's about the total orientation of the self toward the good of others. But becoming familiar with blessings from the Bible is a way of learning and acquiring the language of blessing. Scripture is the richest reserve we have when it comes to finding words to express future good that is in step with God's will. Don't just read these blessings from Paul's letters; it's important to *speak* them. If you're discussing the book with a small group, consider breaking into pairs at the end of your conversation to pray for one another and to practice speaking blessing to one another.

· *Craft a Blessing.* Prompts to craft blessings give you an opportunity to put what you're learning into practice. Composing blessings of your own can enliven your prayers and strengthen your relationships.

While this guide can be used for personal reflection and journaling, it's likely to be most meaningful when shared within a small group.

A note on giving and receiving words of blessing: I know from experience that speaking blessing can be awkward at first. When I began trying to speak blessings to friends while looking them in the eyes, I teared up and my voice trembled, sometimes so much so that I struggled to express even the simplest blessings. But with practice, speaking these meaningful words became more natural, as blessings were impressed into my heart and mind over time.

Blessing is a prayer spoken in the presence of God, but it is communicated to a particular person. Since blessing is a relational form of intercession, attend to and focus on the person with whom you're praying. You may be accustomed to praying with your eyes closed, but it's important for the person receiving a blessing to know they have been seen. So don't be afraid to open your eyes. Try to perceive the image of God in the person you are blessing.

Appropriate touch can also be an important aspect of communicating blessing, so you may want to rest your hand on the person's shoulder or arm while praying. Speak the blessing in love directly to the person you want to bless.

Chapter I:
Blessing in the Beginning: Into Relationship

> Taste and see that the LORD is good;
>   blessed is the one who takes refuge in him.
> PSALM 34:8, NIV

READ
Genesis 1–3; Psalm 103

REFLECT
#Blessed. These days the word *blessed* has become a hashtag, a slogan, a word to calligraphy on canvas or embroider on decorative pillows. Describe your associations with the words *blessed* and *blessing*. Do you shrink from using these words or gravitate toward them? What experiences have most shaped your understanding of the meaning of blessing?

The first time we encounter the word *bless* in the first chapter of Genesis, it's used as a verb, not a noun. How does reading "Be fruitful and multiply" as a blessing, rather than as a command, affect your understanding of God's first interaction with humanity?

"God's blessing is intimately relational because it invites communion." How might thinking of blessing as dialogue and conversation affect the way you pray? How have you experienced the relational dynamic of God's blessing?

If blessing strengthens relationships, sin and the resulting curse fracture them. Have you ever felt the curse of sin

affect one of your close relationships? How have you seen
the effects of curse—tension, discord, distrust, shame,
alienation—manifest in your own life?

Tina describes a sunrise as a moment when she appreciated
the givenness of blessing from God in a way that inspired her
to respond with a blessing. What are some given blessings
that draw you closer to God in praise and thanksgiving?

A BLESSING TO LEARN AND SHARE

> May the God of peace make you holy in every way,
> and may your whole spirit and soul and body be kept
> blameless until our Lord Jesus Christ comes again.
>
> I THESSALONIANS 5:23, NLT

This blessing focuses on the process of sanctification, which
means to be made holy. Sanctification is a blessing that
comes from God alone. When God blessed the seventh day
of Creation, he made it holy (Genesis 2:3). Paul's blessing to
the Thessalonians reminds us that we are created as an integrated whole—spirit, soul, and body. The process of becoming holy involves the whole of our being. The blessing of
holiness has as much an effect on what we do with our bodies as it does on the restoration of our souls. Ask the Lord if
there's someone you know who would be blessed by hearing
these words spoken to them. If you're meeting with a small
group, break into pairs so that each person has an opportunity to receive this blessing and to pray it over someone in
the group.

COMPOSE A BLESSING

The practice of blessing begins with returning blessing to God, the source of all good. Try writing a blessing to God inspired by the ways you've experienced grace in your life. Psalm 103 is a marvelous example of how to relate to God through words of blessing. When we bless our Maker, we praise attributes of his character and thank him for all the good he's given.

Chapter 2:
Blessing That Frees Us to Follow: Letting Go

> Blessed are those whose strength is in you,
>   whose hearts are set on pilgrimage.
>
> PSALM 84:5, NIV

READ

Genesis 11:27–12:9; Matthew 8:18-21; 16:24-25; Luke 14:26-33; Galatians 3:1-9

REFLECT

When you read Genesis 12:1-4, what stands out most to you—the demand of the call or the goodness of the blessing? Why?

If you had been Abraham, how do you think you might have responded to the call to leave your familiar environment and relationships? Would you have been looking at the leaving or toward the blessing? Why?

Jesus said, "Any one of you who does not renounce *all that he has* cannot be my disciple" (Luke 14:33, emphasis added). What are some blessings that you may be grasping for or holding on to? What good things or relationships are you afraid to release to the Lord?

Commenting on the demand of Jesus' call in Luke 14, G. B. Caird explains that "Jesus is not advocating the abandonment of family ties, let alone misanthropy, but is demanding that, where there is a clash of loyalty between the claims of family and the claims of the kingdom of God, the service of the kingdom shall come first."[1] Examining your life, where do you think there might be a clash of loyalties with Jesus' call?

Look again at God's blessing of Abraham in Genesis 12:2-3. Would you classify this blessing as material, spiritual, or both? Why?

Elevating material blessing over spiritual blessing can quickly become dangerous, a prosperity gospel that teaches us to seek a relationship with God because of what's in it for us. Greed is never fertile ground for spiritual growth. But strict asceticism that renounces material blessing—of family and friends, of home and intimacy, of taste and touch—may seem spiritual but denies the goodness of the blessing God meant for us to enjoy. How could we cultivate a healthy gratitude for both material and spiritual blessings?

How have you seen God's blessings of provision, protection, and presence manifested in your life? Which of these dimensions of blessing has been most meaningful to you?

In Galatians 3:8-9, Paul calls the blessing of Abraham the *protevangelion*, or "the gospel beforehand." What aspects of the blessing of Abraham do you associate with the gospel?

What does it mean to you to be adopted into the family called to become a blessing for all families on earth?

A BLESSING TO LEARN AND SHARE

> May God make you worthy of his calling,
> and by his power may he fulfill your every desire for
>   goodness
> and your every deed prompted by faith.
> May the name of our Lord Jesus be glorified in you, and
>   you in him.
>
> 2 THESSALONIANS 1:11-12, AUTHOR'S PARAPHRASE

This blessing focuses on the graciousness of God's calling of each person who believes and finds life in Christ. Just as Abraham was called for a purpose—to become a blessing for all the families of the earth—those called by God are also set apart for good deeds prompted by faith and empowered by God's Spirit. As we desire good and act toward our neighbors in a way that communicates God's goodness, the name of Christ is glorified in us even as we are glorified in him.

COMPOSE A BLESSING

Compose a blessing to someone who has left their comfort zone to serve God—a social worker, a counselor, a pastor, a worship leader, a missionary, a humanitarian-aid worker. Think of the stresses and difficulties that person may deal with on a day-to-day basis. Consider the comforts they let go of and the future good that could sustain them. Write a blessing that encourages dependence on the Lord's power, strength, and goodness.

Chapter 3:
Blessing a Child: Envisioning Future Hope

> Blessed are those whose help is the God of Jacob,
> whose hope is in the LORD their God.
>
> PSALM 146:5, NIV

READ
Genesis 27:1–28:5; 48–49; Hebrews 11:8-22

REFLECT
If "blessing begins with seeing," what makes it difficult for you to focus on those you love so that you see them in a meaningful way?

When you read the story of Isaac's blessing of Jacob and Esau, is there a character in the story you most identify with? Why do you think the blessing broke the family apart? Reflect on a time you experienced or observed manipulation or favoritism in your family.

How do you think underlying motivations for blessing can affect the way a blessing is received and the impact it has on relationships?

Look again at Jacob's blessing of Ephraim and Manasseh in Genesis 48:15-16. Notice that the blessing incorporates personal testimony. Have you ever thought of your testimony as a source of blessing to others? Whose testimony has blessed you by drawing you nearer to God?

"The blessing of our children can't be separated from the vitality of our own relationship with God." Does this insight encourage or discourage you? Why? How do you think words of blessing might be inspired by personal prayer and worship?

Have you ever been given a suitable blessing—a blessing that was written or spoken to you in a particular time or situation? How did it impact you?

A BLESSING TO LEARN AND SHARE

May God fill you with the knowledge of his will
through all wisdom and understanding that the Spirit
    gives,
so that you may live a life worthy of the Lord and please
    him in every way:
bearing fruit in every good work,
and growing in the knowledge of God.

COLOSSIANS 1:9-10, AUTHOR'S PARAPHRASE

Knowledge of God's will through spiritual wisdom and understanding are gifts given by the Holy Spirit as he counsels and comforts us. This blessing connects these good gifts with their purpose—living a life pleasing to the Lord and in service to others. Living with purpose and meaning is a profound blessing. Through this prayer, Paul is reminding the Colossians that faith is not static, that redemption is just the beginning of a journey with God that expands our knowledge of his character. There is a beautiful circularity to this blessing—our knowledge of God motivates our service, and as we bear fruit in every good work, our knowledge of God increases.

COMPOSE A BLESSING

Craft a suitable blessing for a child, teenager, or college student in your family or church community.

- Begin with prayer and worship, asking God to reveal truth to you and to help you see with spiritual vision.

- Jot down qualities you see in the child or student that could be affirmed and developed. Write down both strengths and areas for growth.

- Think about challenges the child is currently facing or might confront in the future, and consider how the blessing might speak to those realities.

- Search Scripture for phrases or verses that could be woven into the blessing. The Psalms and the blessings in Paul's letters are a great source for inspiration.

- Consider incorporating a metaphor that would make the blessing memorable.

- Write the blessing by pulling together these various strands of thought. Let the blessing rest a day or two and then come back to it, editing and revising if necessary. Now read the whole blessing as a prayer, asking God to confirm that these words are suited to this person at this time.

- Share the blessing. You might want to write it in a card or journal so it can be kept and remembered. If you have an opportunity, read the words aloud as a prayer given in relationship.

Chapter 4:
Blessing That Creates Community:
Seeing (and Being) Shine

> Blessed are those who have learned to acclaim you,
>   who walk in the light of your presence, LORD.
>
> PSALM 89:15, NIV

READ

Exodus 34; Numbers 6:22-27; Isaiah 58:6-12, 60;
Matthew 17:1-9; John 1:1-18

REFLECT

Does the church you grew up in or the one you currently
attend end worship with a benediction? How did (or
do) benedictions make you feel? Do you receive them as
blessing, or do they seem like a formality to you? Why?

Look at the three lines of the blessing in Numbers 6.
Which of the lines speaks to you most powerfully? How do
the lines relate to each other?

This chapter delves into the meaning of experiencing the
"shine" of God's face, but the promise of God's favor is
also an important aspect of the blessing. Read Exodus
33:12-16. What does it reveal about the meaning of the
Lord's favor?

Try to imagine the experience of witnessing the shine on
Moses' face described in Exodus 34:29-35 and the shine of
the Transfiguration of Jesus described in Matthew 17:1-9.

What are similarities and dissimilarities about these two instances of shine? What do they reveal to you about being in God's presence?

In what ways have you experienced the blessing of God's shine in your life? (You might refer to 2 Corinthians 4:6 and 2 Peter 1:16-19 for a hint.)

Have you ever been hesitant to bless another person because you felt you lacked the spiritual authority to do so? How does the insight drawn from 1 Peter 2:4-9—that in Christ, we are both family and a royal priesthood—affect your freedom to bless others?

Tina describes being drawn to the shine she experienced at her friend Mary Jo's table. Who has mediated God's shine to you in spiritual and practical ways?

With Isaiah 58 and 60 in mind, how do you think reflecting God's shine affects our mission in the world?

A BLESSING TO LEARN AND SHARE

May the God of our Lord Jesus Christ, the glorious Father,
give you the Spirit of wisdom and revelation so that you may know him better.
May the eyes of your heart be enlightened so that you may know the hope of your calling.

EPHESIANS 1:17-18, AUTHOR'S PARAPHRASE

Shine is the physical manifestation of God's glory. In this blessing, Paul identifies God as the *glorious* Father who reveals himself by sending his Spirit, the source of wisdom and insight, to enlighten the eyes of our hearts. The metaphor of spiritual eyes that are wide open and able to perceive God's shine stands in stark contrast to the blindness of those who worship idols rather than the living God (Isaiah 44:9-20) or the blindness of legalists who emphasize outward compliance with tradition rather than a vital relationship with God that includes internal purity of heart (Matthew 15:1-20). This blessing suggests that as our hearts are illuminated by the Spirit, we are filled with the eternal hope that invigorates those called into relationship with God.

COMPOSE A BLESSING

Write a blessing for someone who has mediated God's grace to you. Reflect on the ways they've served you or the ways you've observed them serving the body of Christ. Express your gratitude for their faithfulness while encouraging them to press on. Consider complementing a written or spoken blessing with an act of service. Often, those who pour themselves out for others don't have a regular experience of people pouring into them. Surprise them with a meal, an invitation to watch their kids so they can go see a movie, or some other unexpected kindness.

Chapter 5:
Inspiration for Blessing: Beyond Magic

> Blessed is the one
>> who trusts in the LORD,
> who does not look to the proud,
>> to those who turn aside to false gods.
>
> PSALM 40:4, NIV

READ

Numbers 22–24; Psalm 13; James 3:2-12

REFLECT

Dallas Willard explains curse as "the projection of evil on someone." It may be expressed verbally or nonverbally. Have you ever sensed that someone was interacting with you in a way that communicated a desire to tear you down? What form did the curse take? How did you respond?

If you were to ask family or friends whether you communicate blessing or curse more often, what do you think they would say?

Rather than dismissing or suppressing the pain caused by interpersonal conflict, it's important to express hurt in a healthy way. Psalms of lament (for example, Psalm 6, 13, 35, 42, 43, and 55) demonstrate how we can bring our hurt, frustration, and fear to God. How is lamentation an expression of faith? If lamentation has helped you process a broken relationship, describe the effect it had and how you saw God work through the situation.

In Turkish culture, nazar boncuk are charms used to guard against the curse of the evil eye. Can you describe a way in which blessing or cursing sometimes acquires a magical dimension in the culture in which you live? Reflect on how Christian blessing is different from the practice of blessing we sometimes observe in other religions.

"The inspiration for blessing comes from two primary sources: God's Word and the indwelling of God's Spirit." In Romans 8:26-27, Paul says that the Spirit helps us pray in accordance with the will of God. If you struggle to think of words that will be a blessing, how can you seek the Holy Spirit for counsel and guidance? Can you remember and describe an instance when God's Word or God's Spirit inspired you to bless someone?

Have you ever noticed the blessings woven through the book of Ruth before? Does it surprise you that a person from a nation judged by God could also be blessed and redeemed by him? How can you see the gospel in this story?

"God's blessing is never—*never ever*—for sale. If you could buy blessing, then it would be a transaction, not a gift." Have you ever attempted to buy a blessing from God? How has your longing for blessing been intertwined with your fears?

A BLESSING TO LEARN AND SHARE

May God strengthen you with power through his Spirit in your inner being,

> so that Christ may dwell in your hearts through faith.
> May you, being rooted and grounded in love,
> have power, together with all the Lord's holy people,
> to grasp how wide and long and high and deep is the
>   love of Christ,
> and to know this love that surpasses knowledge.
> EPHESIANS 3:16-19, AUTHOR'S PARAPHRASE

This blessing focuses on the unfathomable dimensions of God's love. There's an intriguing tension between being stabilized by—rooted and grounded in—a love that's too expansive to fully know. Paul suggests we only begin to grasp the extent of God's love when we are together with all the Lord's people. Gathering for fellowship, worship, and service with other believers is where we begin understanding the depth of God's love for us. This blessing, then, finds its richest expression within the church. It's a blessing for a community.

COMPOSE A BLESSING

Ruth was a foreigner, but Naomi, Boaz, and the community reached out to her with blessing. Think of someone you know who seems like an outsider in your community—an immigrant or refugee, an international student, or someone who recently moved to town and doesn't yet have many local friends. Write a blessing that expresses the goodness of welcome. Consider sharing it with this individual or family. Complement the blessing with an invitation to share a cup of tea or coffee or a meal in your home.

Chapter 6:
Sustaining Blessing: When Life Is Hard

> Yet the LORD longs to be gracious to you;
>   therefore he will rise up to show you compassion.
> For the LORD is a God of justice.
>   Blessed are all who wait for him!
>
> ISAIAH 30:18, NIV

READ

Genesis 17:15-21; 18:1-15; 21:1-7; Isaiah 61; Matthew 5:1-11; Luke 1–2

REFLECT

What qualities do you usually associate with a "blessed" life? How does Mary's life (see Luke 1) challenge your expectations of what it means to be blessed by God?

If you've ever experienced blessing through suffering and loss, how did God manifest his presence to you and sustain you?

Have you been tempted to think that some things may be too hard for the Lord? Have you ever waited so long for God to fulfill a promise that you felt hope evaporating? How does Sarah and Abraham's story challenge you to be faithful in waiting for God to act?

In what way could Simeon's prophetic word to Mary that "a sword will pierce your own soul" be understood as a blessing?

"Sorrow *isn't* blessing, but the healing presence of the Lord in the midst of sorrow *is* a profound blessing." Reflect on and describe a time when you experienced the blessing of the Lord's presence during a painful time when you felt poor in spirit or when you were mourning and in need of comfort.

If you've never thought about the reality that the son Mary carried in her womb was the same one who welcomed her into an eternal home, how do you react to the image of Mary's soul safe in the arms of the Son who had become her Redeemer?

The grace of giving blessing is balanced by opening ourselves to the grace of receiving blessing. That's especially true when we're suffering. Are you more comfortable giving blessing than you are receiving it? Why? How can you be more open to receiving blessing?

A BLESSING TO LEARN AND SHARE

May the God of hope fill you with all joy and peace in
believing,
so that by the power of the Holy Spirit you may
[overflow] with hope.
ROMANS 15:13

Mary was most blessed because she "believed that there would be a fulfillment of what was spoken to her from the Lord" (Luke 1:45). As a theological virtue, hope is found at the intersection of desire for good and the expectation of receiving it; and so, it is rightly paired with the blessing of believing. Hope is like an inoculation against despair; it bookends Paul's blessing, which begins with God as the source of hope and concludes with the image of a heart so full of hope that it overflows. Earlier (Romans 5:1-5), Paul explains that hope is a gift of the Holy Spirit that is poured into our hearts when we find peace with God through Jesus Christ.

COMPOSE A BLESSING

Think of someone who is walking through dark days, someone struggling through a painful conflict or an unexpected loss, someone so consumed by present difficulty that they may be tempted to despair. Pray that the Spirit of the Lord would counsel and direct you to speak a blessing or serve in a way that would communicate hope to this person. Write a blessing that affirms they are seen and loved while navigating this painful season. Imagine the warmth of the sunrise after a long, cold night, and ask the Lord for hope to dawn and bring healing in its wings (Malachi 4:2).

Chapter 7:
Blessing around the Table: Shared Abundance

> Blessed is he who comes in the name of the LORD.
> From the house of the LORD we bless you.
>
> PSALM 118:26, NIV

READ

Matthew 26:17-29; Luke 9:10-20; 10:1-24; 24:36-53;
John 6:1-59

REFLECT

In her book *Daring Greatly*, Brené Brown notes that a
fear of scarcity—of never having enough—has taken hold
in American culture. How does Jesus' feeding of the five
thousand challenge a scarcity mind-set? Have you ever
been in a situation when the need exceeded the material
resources on hand, but God provided in an unexpectedly
abundant way? If so, reflect on what you learned through
the experience.

Describe your experiences of blessing before a meal.
Do prayers associated with eating feel routine, or are
they meaningful for you? Why? How might blessings
around the table acquire deeper meaning for you and
your family?

Why do you think the feeding of the five thousand may
have been the only miracle other than the Resurrection
that was recorded by all four Gospel writers? Explain the

significance of this miracle for your understanding of
Jesus' identity.

Think of the images of Jesus you grew up seeing. What
impression did they give you? How do you react to the
image of Jesus with his hand raised in a gesture of blessing?

Consider the relationship between blessing and
commissioning. Claus Westermann suggests that by
bestowing his blessing, Jesus is leaving power with his
disciples. Have you ever associated power with a blessing?
Why or why not?

Remember that Abraham was called with the promise
that through his family, all the families on earth will be
blessed. Discuss how Jesus' sending of his disciples into
the world with a blessing of peace might be related to that
promise.

A BLESSING TO LEARN AND SHARE

> May our Lord Jesus Christ himself and God our Father,
>   who loved us and by his grace gave us eternal
>   encouragement and good hope, encourage your
>   hearts and strengthen you in every good deed and
>   word. . . .
> May the Lord direct your hearts into God's love and
>   Christ's perseverance.

2 THESSALONIANS 2:16-17; 3:5, NIV

Good deeds *and* words—this blessing reminds us that God strengthens and encourages us to share both. There's no conflict between blessing through words, witness, and acts of mercy because all testify to the grace and eternal hope we've received through Jesus Christ. Paul makes it clear that although we're not saved *by* our works, we are saved *"for* good works, which God prepared beforehand, that we should walk in them" (Ephesians 2:10, emphasis added). Both our words and deeds should be inspired by God's love and reflect Christ's perseverance, the resolve to keep loving and doing good even when it's painful, even when our kindness and care are not returned.

COMPOSE A BLESSING

We focused on two aspects of God's blessing in this chapter— abundant provision in the face of scarcity and abundant peace that flows from reconciliation with God. Think of someone you know who struggles with a scarcity mind-set, who tends to think there's never enough to go around, or someone plagued with anxiety, uncertainty, or fear. Write and share a blessing that calls to mind the one who can do exceedingly more than we ask or expect (Ephesians 3:20). Reflect, too, on the warning of James 2:14 that speaking a blessing without providing for a physical need we could meet is fruitless. Are you aware of a need in your community or in the world that you have the capacity and resources to meet? How might the Lord be prompting you to respond in a way that reflects the peace of the Lord?

Chapter 8:
Blessing Even Enemies: The Arena of Grace

> Show me the wonders of your great love,
>   you who save by your right hand
>   those who take refuge in you from their foes.
> Keep me as the apple of your eye;
>   hide me in the shadow of your wings.
>
> PSALM 17:7-8, NIV

READ
Matthew 5–7; Luke 6:29-49; Romans 5:6-10; 12:9-21;
1 Peter 2:11-25; 3:8-17

REFLECT
How have you seen reciprocity and retribution play into
your relationships with friends and family? How could
Jesus' teaching to bless those who curse and do good to
those who hate disrupt unhealthy patterns that may have
defined some of your relationships?

If you're reluctant to live in the relational space Jesus is
defining in the Sermon on the Mount—to enter the arena
of grace—what is the source of your hesitation?

How does understanding Jesus' call to love our enemies
as an aspect of *common grace* that reflects the mercy of
God poured out even on the undeserving (Luke 6:35-36)
help you make sense of the call to bless those who curse?
Does knowing that Jesus calls his followers to bless in this
inclusive way seem like good or bad news to you? Why?

"To bless those who curse is to extend *unmerited* favor, *undeserved* mercy, *unearned* grace." Have you ever been on the receiving end of this kind of blessing? How did it make you feel?

Have you ever seen love expressed toward an enemy break a cycle of hurt and bring reconciliation? If so, describe what you learned from the experience.

Is there anyone you feel unable to love and incapable of praying for? How might meditating on Jesus' example of loving us even when we were his enemies, described by Paul in Romans 5:6-11, help reorient your heart?

A BLESSING TO LEARN AND SHARE

May the Lord make your love increase and overflow for each other and for everyone you meet.
May the Lord strengthen your heart so that you will be blameless and holy in the presence of our God and Father.

I THESSALONIANS 3:12-13, AUTHOR'S PARAPHRASE

The language of Paul's blessings is bold. His prayers are staggeringly ambitious. He doesn't pray we'll have a little bit more love for others; he prays we will be filled with so much love that it can't be contained. He doesn't pray that the love in our hearts will be ladled out to a few; he prays that it will flow out to *everyone*—every single person that we meet. God's love is boundless, capable of transcending the bounds of human vulnerability and moral weakness. None of us is capable of living up to this blessing in our own strength. Paul is giving us a vision of what is possible when the supernatural love of God fills us and transforms us from flawed to forgiven, from filthy to cleansed, from fallen to redeemed. That's why the blessing of overflowing love is given beside the blessing of strength of heart and holiness. When we come into God's presence, we're positioning ourselves to receive love and grace from his hands, blessings that flow through us like living water.

COMPOSE A BLESSING

There is no more difficult call than to love those who hate, no more unnatural response than blessing those who curse; and yet, that's what Jesus asks us to do. When you think of the word *enemy*, who comes to mind? Whose presence tends to provoke anger? Whom do you avoid running into or relating to whenever possible? Whose memory or appearance is most attached to feelings of pain? Spend some time with the Lord in prayer, asking him to cleanse you of any bitterness in your heart toward your enemy and give you the resolve to overcome evil with good. Ask him to love through you in a supernatural way that reflects the mercy of Christ. Try writing a blessing for that person that demonstrates an authentic desire for him or her to experience God's goodness, mercy, and grace.

Chapter 9:
Blessing That Cancels Curse: The Living Tree

> Blessed is the one
>   whose transgressions are forgiven,
>   whose sins are covered.
> Blessed is the one
>   whose sin the LORD does not count against them
>   and in whose spirit is no deceit.
>
> PSALM 32:1-2, NIV

READ

Deuteronomy 11:26-32; 27–30; Acts 5:27-42; Galatians 3

REFLECT

Describe your associations with the cross and Jesus'
crucifixion. How does grasping the early Christian
perception of the cross as a symbol of curse expand your
understanding of the meaning of Jesus' death on a tree?

Read Deuteronomy 11:26-32. Note the differences between
Mount Gerizim and Mount Ebal—which is associated with
blessing and which with curse? Now look at Deuteronomy
27:1-8. On which mountain does Moses say the stones with
the words of the law written on them should be set up? Why
do you think this detail is significant?

Since the covenant ceremony described in Deuteronomy
27–30 was made between God and the nation of
Israel, can you understand why keeping the law was a

life-or-death matter for Jews in Jesus' day? What was the ultimate expectation to which the prophetic word given in Deuteronomy 30:1-6 points?

How does grasping the weight of the threat of curse in Deuteronomy help you understand what Paul is saying in Galatians 3:10-14 about Jesus becoming a curse for us to free us from the curse of the law?

Have you ever felt the moral demands of the law were too much for you to bear? How does appreciating that Jesus "redeemed us from that self-defeating, cursed life by absorbing it completely into himself" (Galatians 3:13, MSG) free you to live in God's blessing?

In Galatians 3:7-9, Paul says clearly that through Christ, the Gentiles—those who are not ethnically Jewish or biologically related to Abraham—can be blessed along with Abraham. Reread the original blessing to Abraham in Genesis 12:2-3. What was the purpose for which Abraham was blessed? If you've been grafted into the family of Abraham by faith, how might being incorporated into the family God has blessed for a particular purpose give your life meaning?

A BLESSING TO LEARN AND SHARE

May you be encouraged in heart and united in love,
so that you may have the full riches of
understanding,

> in order that you may know the mystery of God,
>   namely, Christ,
> in whom are hidden all the treasures of wisdom and
>   knowledge.
>
> COLOSSIANS 2:2-3, AUTHOR'S PARAPHRASE

When an implement of torture and a symbol of curse is transformed into a means of grace and a symbol of blessing, that's a profound mystery. Mysterious, too, is the way that Christ could take on himself—*in* himself—the sin and curse of the whole world. But it is this mystery that is at the heart of Christianity. This blessing focuses on the treasures of wisdom and knowledge that are, paradoxically, both hidden and revealed in Christ, who was "the image of the invisible God" (Colossians 1:15). This wisdom is bound to appear foolish in the eyes of secularized skeptics, but the mystery of Christ—the only one in whom "the fullness of God was pleased to dwell," the one who made "peace by the blood of his cross" (Colossians 1:19-20)—is, for those who believe, the source of eternal life, reconciliation, and truth.

COMPOSE A BLESSING

As you reflect on the mystery of the cross, pray that the Lord would call to mind someone you know who may be alienated from God because of unresolved questions about the identity of Jesus and the truth of Scripture. Think of someone you're acquainted with who may associate Christian faith more with foolishness than wisdom. Pray that in the light of Christ, the fog of doubt would dissipate.

Write and pray a blessing that conveys hope of clarity, the treasure of wisdom, and the goodness of knowledge that is revealed by the Spirit. Ask the Lord to give you discernment about how and when to share the hope that you've found in Christ.

Chapter 10:
Transformation: Wrestling for Blessing

> Come, you who are blessed by my Father, inherit the
> kingdom prepared for you from the foundation of
> the world.
>
> MATTHEW 25:34

READ
Genesis 28:10-22; 32; Ezekiel 47:1-12;
Ephesians 1:3-14; Revelation 22

REFLECT
Since a series of blessings helped transform Jacob from a
taker and deceiver into a giver, how might you anticipate
God's blessing working in your own heart? What are some
blessings that have helped refine your character?

Have you ever sensed that your devotion to God was
conditional or that you were wrestling with God for a
blessing? What was the result? Was there resolution, or
is the struggle ongoing? What can you learn from Jacob's
prayer in Genesis 32:9-12?

Consider and discuss what it might mean that the name
Israel means one who strives with God.

What aspect of John's vision of an era of blessing in
Revelation 22:1-5 most excites you? Why?

What are some of the challenges of living suspended between a blessing already realized in Christ and a state of blessing anticipated but not yet fulfilled?

How does understanding the way blessing is threaded through the Bible from Genesis to Revelation change your perception of the purpose of your life? Who are you perfectly positioned to bless?

A BLESSING TO LEARN AND SHARE

> May the grace of the Lord Jesus Christ,
> and the steadfast love of God,
> and the fellowship of the Holy Spirit be with you.
>
> 2 CORINTHIANS 13:14, AUTHOR'S PARAPHRASE

The grace that rescues us, the steadfast love that sustains us, the fellowship that knits us into a community of faith—I cannot imagine a more profound blessing than this. This benediction evokes the abiding presence of the Trinity, one God in three persons. It is a succinct summary of the gospel—that we are invited to experience the love of God and fellowship through the Spirit by grace offered to us in Jesus' life, death, and resurrection. And it is a heartfelt petition that you would never be alone, but that God would be *with you*. The central marvel of the revelation that unfolds in the pages of Scripture is that we are not alone in the world. We are known, we are loved, we are blessed, and we are being welcomed into the presence of God and into the family related to him. May this grace, this love, this fellowship be with you all.

notes

CHAPTER I: BLESSING IN THE BEGINNING

1. *Online Etymology Dictionary*, s.v. "congratulation (n.)," accessed December 12, 2018, https://www.etymonline.com/word/congratulation.
2. John O'Donohue, *To Bless the Space Between Us: A Book of Blessings* (New York: Doubleday, 2008), 217.
3. Gordon J. Wenham, *Word Biblical Commentary*, vol. 1, *Genesis 1-15* (Waco, TX: Word Books, 1987), 275.
4. Claus Westermann, *Genesis 1-11: A Continental Commentary* (Minneapolis: Fortress, 1994), 161.
5. Walter Brueggemann, *The Prophetic Imagination*, 2nd ed. (Minneapolis: Fortress, 2001), 14.
6. Jacques Ellul, *The Humiliation of the Word* (Grand Rapids, MI: Eerdmans, 1985), 50–51. Emphasis added.
7. Bruce K. Waltke with Cathi J. Fredricks, *Genesis: A Commentary* (Grand Rapids, MI: Zondervan, 2001), 94.
8. John Milton, *Paradise Lost: A Poem in Twelve Books* (London: Chiswick, 1823), 232, 235. Emphasis added.
9. Aaron Hubbell, "'Things Not Seen' in the Frescoes of Giotto: An Analysis of Illusory and Spiritual Depth" (master's thesis, Louisiana State University, 2017), 31–32, https://digitalcommons.lsu.edu/cgi/viewcontent.cgi?article =5409&context=gradschool_theses.
10. G. K. Chesterton, *Saint Francis of Assisi* (Peabody, MA: Hendrickson, 2008), 70.
11. John Tolan, *Saint Francis and the Sultan: The Curious History of a Christian-Muslim Encounter* (Oxford: Oxford University Press, 2009), 7–31. Some of de Vitry's reflections on this encounter were recorded in *Historia occidentalis* (written around 1223).
12. Thomas Merton, *The New Man* (London: Burns & Oates, 2003), 6–7. Emphasis added.

CHAPTER 2: BLESSING THAT FREES US TO FOLLOW

1. Walter Brueggemann, *Genesis* (Atlanta: John Knox, 1982), 118.
2. In Genesis 12:1, the Hebrew word used for "kindred" is *moledheth* (https://www.biblestudytools.com/dictionary/kindred/) and the words used for "father's house" are *ābîkā ūmibbêt* (https://biblehub.com/interlinear/genesis/12.htm).
3. Esther de Waal, *The Celtic Way of Prayer: The Recovery of the Religious Imagination* (New York: Doubleday, 1997), 5; de Waal is quoting from Nora Chadwick, *The Age of the Saints in the Early Celtic Church* (London: Oxford University Press, 1961), 64.
4. de Waal, *Celtic Way of Prayer*, 1–9.
5. For context, see also Matthew 8:18-20; 10:37; 16:24-25; Luke 14:26-33. "Jesus is not advocating the abandonment of family ties, let alone misanthropy, but is demanding that, where there is a clash of loyalty between the claims of family and the claims of the kingdom of God, the service of the kingdom shall come first." G. B. Caird, *The Language and Imagery of the Bible* (Philadelphia: Westminster, 1980), 111.
6. Simone Weil, *Waiting for God*, trans. Emma Craufurd (New York: Harper Collins, 2001), 73.
7. John Piper, *Future Grace* (Sisters, OR: Multnomah, 1995), 18.
8. For the five blessings prior to Genesis 12, see Genesis 1:22, 28; 2:3; 5:2; 9:1. For the five after, see Genesis 18:18; 22:18; 26:2-5 (to Isaac); 28:14 (to Jacob). Bruce K. Waltke with Cathi J. Fredricks, *Genesis: A Commentary* (Grand Rapids, MI: Zondervan, 2001), 203, 205.
9. I credit Ken Hemphill for suggesting these three points. I heard him preach a sermon years ago on this passage, and when I was working on this chapter, he reminded me of the way he had characterized God's blessing as provision, protection, and presence.
10. See also Genesis 27:29; Numbers 24:9. Waltke, *Genesis*, 206.
11. John Calvin, quoted in Waltke, *Genesis*, 205. Emphasis added.
12. *Brown-Driver-Briggs Hebrew and English Lexicon, Unabridged*, s.v. "berakah," accessed December 12, 2018, https://biblehub.com/hebrew/1293.htm.
13. When I wrote this text, I wasn't aware that Derek Kidner makes a similar comparison in *Genesis: An Introduction and Commentary*, Tyndale Old Testament Commentaries (Downers Grove, IL: InterVarsity, 1967), 70.
14. Waltke, *Genesis*, 209.
15. *Merriam-Webster*, s.v. "protevangelium," accessed December 12, 2018, https://www.merriam-webster.com/dictionary/protevangelium.
16. "To live in that [God's] atmosphere is what we're asking in a blessing. We're asking for an entire atmosphere of God's reality to be present on the person we are blessing under the invocation of God." Dallas Willard, *Living in Christ's Presence: Final Words on Heaven and the Kingdom of God* (Downers Grove, IL: InterVarsity, 2014), 167.

CHAPTER 3: BLESSING A CHILD

1. *Holman Bible Dictionary*, s.v. "Birthright," accessed November 27, 2018, https://www.studylight.org/dictionaries/hbd/b/birthright.html.
2. "This narrative assumes and affirms that *spoken words shape human life.* Language is not simply an exercise in propaganda and manipulation (as it tends to be in our modern world). Words here are not a matter of indifference which may be attended to or not, as is convenient. Here, when words are spoken by authoritative persons in proper contexts, they have a substance. . . . They must be handled with respect, for they are means toward life or death (cf. James 3:10)." Walter Brueggemann, *Genesis* (Atlanta: John Knox, 1982), 228. Emphasis in original.
3. See Genesis 31:36-41.
4. *Jacob*: A footnote to Genesis 25:26 (NIV) explains, "*Jacob* means *he grasps the heel*, a Hebrew idiom for *he deceives.*" *Israel*: "This name is a combination of the Hebrew words for "wrestle" and "God." *Baker's Evangelical Dictionary of Biblical Theology*, s.v. "Israel," accessed November 27, 2018, https://www.biblestudytools.com/dictionary/israel/.
5. John O'Donohue, *To Bless the Space Between Us: A Book of Blessings* (New York: Doubleday, 2008), 80–81.
6. My kids receive blessings throughout the year. I try to write a blessing for each of them on New Year's Day and for each of their birthdays. Daily blessings are also part of their life.
7. John Trent and Gary Smalley, *The Blessing: Giving the Gift of Unconditional Love and Acceptance* (Nashville: Thomas Nelson, 2011), 46–47. Emphasis added. Trent and Smalley's book focuses on five critical aspects of blessing within the family—meaningful touch, a spoken message, attaching high value, picturing a special future, and an active commitment to seeing the blessing realized.
8. See James Montgomery Boice, *Genesis: An Expositional Commentary*, vol. 3, *Genesis 37–50* (Grand Rapids, MI: Baker, 1998), 1154–229, for an exposition of the meaning of each prophecy with attention to fulfillment in the life of Jesus and application to the lives of Christians.
9. Eugene Peterson, *The Jesus Way: A Conversation on the Ways That Jesus Is the Way* (Grand Rapids, MI: Eerdmans, 2011), 25.
10. Mircea Eliade, *Images and Symbols: Studies in Religious Symbolism*, trans. Philip Mairet (Princeton, NJ: Princeton University Press, 1991), 20.
11. Bruce K. Waltke with Cathi J. Fredricks, *Genesis: A Commentary* (Grand Rapids, MI: Zondervan, 2001), 603.
12. Waltke, *Genesis*, 603. Emphasis added.

CHAPTER 4: BLESSING THAT CREATES COMMUNITY

1. The Rabbi Hayim Halevy Donin observes that the blessing "took place every day, immediately following the daily morning offering. . . . But

the blessing did not stay confined to the Temple. It became part of communal prayer assemblies even before there was a synagogue, and then was incorporated into the ritual of the synagogue." Rabbi Hayim Halevy Donin, *To Pray as a Jew: A Guide to the Prayer Book and the Synagogue Service* (New York: Basic Books, 1980), 133.

2. "The highlight of the [temple] service was the pronouncement of the unspoken name of God, the 'tetragrammaton' (i.e., the four sacred letters YHWH), which is repeated three times in the Aaronic benediction. And on hearing the tetragrammaton thrice-repeated, the crowds fell and hid their faces as a reverential act in the presence of the holy." Asher Finkel, "Prayer in Jewish Life of the First Century as Background to Early Christianity," in *Into God's Presence: Prayer in the New Testament*, ed. Richard N. Longenecker (Grand Rapids, MI: Eerdmans, 2001), 47.

3. "The main themes of the Transfiguration exegesis before the sixth century in both East and the West focused on the Transfiguration as a theophany and as a revelation of the inner life of God; as an event related to the Resurrection; as a prefiguring of the Second Coming; and as a guarantee for the unity and continuity of the two Testaments." Andreas Andreopoulos, *Metamorphosis: The Transfiguration in Byzantine Theology and Iconography* (Crestwood, NY: St. Vladimir's Seminary Press, 2005), 41–42, 133.

4. Leon Morris, *The Gospel according to John*, rev. ed., New International Commentary on the New Testament (Grand Rapids, MI: Eerdmans, 1995), 75. Morris notes that *shines* is the only present-tense verb used in the entire prologue of the book of John, which spans eighteen verses (see John 1:1-18).

5. Morris, *Gospel according to John*, 92–93.

6. "In the NT, Hebrews refers directly to the OT blessing of people through people (Heb. 7:6f.; 11:20f.). Jesus himself obligated his disciples— differently than in the OT—only to bless, not to curse. This directive (Lk. 6:28 par.) finds its way into parenesis (Rom. 12:14; 1 Cor. 4:12; 1 Peter 3:9). Giving blessing, moreover, is now no longer, as in the later layers of the OT and Judaism, the special right of the priests . . . but is assigned to all as a charge." Leonhard Goppelt, *A Commentary on 1 Peter*, trans. John E. Alsup (Grand Rapids, MI: Eerdmans, 1993), 235. Emphasis added.

7. Amy Carmichael, *Gold by Moonlight* (London: SPCK, 1960), 73.

CHAPTER 5: INSPIRATION FOR BLESSING

1. Dallas Willard, *Living in Christ's Presence: Final Words on Heaven and the Kingdom of God* (Downer's Grove, IL: InterVarsity, 2014), 164.

2. See, for instance, Psalm 6, 13, 35, 42, 43, 55.

3. See 1 Samuel 28; 1 Kings 18; 2 Kings 21:1-6.

4. Gordon J. Wenham, *Numbers*, Tyndale Old Testament Commentaries (Downers Grove, IL: InterVarsity, 2008), 168.
5. See Numbers 31:16; 2 Peter 2:15; Revelation 2:14.
6. John O'Donohue, *To Bless the Space Between Us: A Book of Blessings* (New York: Doubleday, 2008), 198.
7. To read more about the Moabite practice of human sacrifice, see Barnes' Notes on the Bible for 2 Kings 3:27, accessed December 13, 2018, https:// biblehub.com/commentaries/2_kings/3-27.htm.
8. See Ruth 1:22; 2:2, 6, 12; 4:5, 10.
9. See Ruth 1:8-17; 2:12; 3:10; 4:11-12.
10. "Büyükada—The Monastery of St. George Koudonas," *Adalar Turizm*, accessed December 13, 2018, https://www.adalarturizm.org/cms/en /component/k2/item/115-bueyuekada-the-monastery-of-st-george -koudonas.
11. D. A. Carson, *A Call to Spiritual Reformation: Priorities from Paul and His Prayers* (Grand Rapids, MI: Baker Academic, 1992), 61.
12. Claus Westermann, *Blessing in the Bible and the Life of the Church* (Philadelphia: Fortress, 1978), 119.

CHAPTER 6: SUSTAINING BLESSING
1. Frederick Buechner, *Telling the Truth: The Gospel as Tragedy, Comedy, and Fairy Tale* (San Francisco: Harper Collins, 1977), 56.
2. Walter Brueggemann, *Genesis* (Atlanta: John Knox, 1982), 159.
3. *NAS Exhaustive Concordance of the Bible with Hebrew-Aramaic and Greek Dictionaries*, s.v. "Yitschaq," accessed November 28, 2018, https://biblehub .com/hebrew/3327.htm.
4. "Pneumonia: The Deadliest Childhood Disease," infographic, UNICEF, accessed December 13, 2018, https://data.unicef.org/wp-content/uploads /2015/12/World-Pneumonia-Day-Infographic_242.pdf.
5. *Strong's Concordance*, s.v. "makarios," accessed December 13, 2018, https:// biblehub.com/greek/3107.htm.
6. See Susan E. Schreiner on Martin Luther's interpretation of the Sermon on the Mount in *The Sermon on the Mount through the Centuries: From the Early Church to John Paul II*, ed. Jeffrey P. Greenman, Timothy Larsen, and Stephen R. Spencer (Grand Rapids, MI: Brazos Press, 2007), 110.
7. The Greek word translated as "comfort" here is *nacham*. See *NAS Old Testament Hebrew Lexicon*, s.v. "Nacham," Bible Study Tools, accessed December 13, 2018, https://www.biblestudytools.com/lexicons/hebrew /nas/nacham.html.
8. Since first seeing this mosaic with my friend Claire, I've read quite a bit about the dormition of the Virgin Mary. A good source for understanding the variations between the three main early Christian traditions regarding the moment when Mary's body and soul are reunited in paradise is

Stephen J. Shoemaker, *Ancient Traditions of the Virgin Mary's Dormition and Assumption* (New York: Oxford University Press, 2002)—Palm traditions, 32–46; Bethlehem traditions, 46–57; Coptic traditions, 58–63.

9. Søren Kierkegaard, *Fear and Trembling* and *The Book on Adler*, trans. Walter Lowrie (New York: Knopf, 1994), 56. Emphasis added.

10. See Psalm 36, 57, 91.

11. *Shield*: Psalm 3, 18, 28; *Rock*: Psalm 18, 62, 95; *Warrior*: Psalm 3, 24, 144.

CHAPTER 7: BLESSING AROUND THE TABLE

1. Matthew 14:13-21; Mark 6:30-44; Luke 9:10-17; John 6:1-14.

2. Rabbi Hayim Halevy Donin, *To Pray as a Jew: A Guide to the Prayer Book and Synagogue Service* (New York: Basic Books, 1980), 65–67, 284–306.

3. Asher Finkel, "Prayer in Jewish Life of the First Century as Background to Early Christianity," in *Into God's Presence: Prayer in the New Testament*, ed. Richard N. Longenecker (Grand Rapids, MI: Eerdmans, 2001), 50.

4. Donin, *To Pray as a Jew*, 289.

5. Donin, *To Pray as a Jew*, 305.

6. Matthew 14:20; Mark 6:42; Luke 9:17.

7. In 1 Corinthians 11:23-26, Paul describes the central importance and symbolic meaning of the Lord's Supper for Christian communities. He ascribes the words "This is my body, broken for you" (MSG) to Jesus.

8. "For the significance of the story we must bear in mind that the figure of eating and drinking is widely used in the Old Testament. It is a figure of prosperity ('nothing is better for a man under the sun than to eat and drink and be glad'; Eccl. 8:15; cf. also Eccl. 3:13; 5:18), and it is often used of the blessings the people of God would enjoy in the promised land (Deut. 8:9; 11:15; Neh. 9:36, etc.)." Leon Morris, *The Gospel According to John* (Grand Rapids, MI: Eerdmans, 1995), 301.

9. "In the New Testament the decisive change was that the blessing of Yahweh, the God of Israel, became blessing in Christ. Christ himself became the one who blesses, and all of God's bestowal of blessing became connected with God's work in Christ." Claus Westermann, *Blessing in the Bible and the Life of the Church* (Philadelphia: Fortress, 1978), 65.

10. I wrote about this in several blog posts: "How the Meaning of the Hagia Sophia Made Me Rethink My New Year's Resolution," December 30, 2017, https://tinaboesch.com/2017/12/30/how-the-meaning-of-the-hagia-sophia-made-me-rethink-my-new-years-resolution/, and—in more depth—in "Veneration Is Not Humiliation: A Theological Interpretation of the Mosaic Over the Imperial Door of the Hagia Sophia," October 31, 2015, https://tinaboesch.com/2015/10/31/a-picture-of-orthodoxy/. This article was originally published in *CRUX* 48, vol. 4 (winter 2013). *CRUX* is a quarterly journal of Christian thought and opinion published by

faculty and alumni of Regent College, Vancouver, which is associated with the University of British Columbia.

11. *Blessing the children*: Luke 18:15-17; *Blessing the meal*: Luke 9:12-16; *Blessing before mission*: Luke 10:1-9; *Blessing during ascension*: Luke 24:50-51.

12. *Englishman's Concordance*, s.v. "eulogein," accessed December 14, 2017, https://biblehub.com/greek/eulogein_2127.htm.

13. Westermann, *Blessing in the Bible*, 69: "The original Greek meaning, 'to use beautiful language,' is found in the New Testament only in Romans 16:18. In all other instances the New Testament concept goes back to the Septuagint usage of *eulogein*, which was intended to render the Hebrew *brk*."

14. Paul J. Achtemeier, *1 Peter: A Commentary*, Hermeneia (Minneapolis: Fortress, 1996), 224.

15. Westermann, *Blessing in the Bible*, 88.

CHAPTER 8: BLESSING EVEN ENEMIES

1. "The Epistle of Polycarp to the Philippians," in *The Apostolic Fathers*, ed. Anthony UYI (Ontario: Devoted Publishing, 2018), 38.

2. "Demolitions Reveal Ancient Roman Theater in Aegean Town," *Hurriyet Daily News*, June 23, 2014, accessed April 11, 2018, http://www .hurriyetdailynews.com/demolitions-reveal-ancient-roman-theater-in -aegean-town--68118.

3. "The Martyrdom of Polycarp," in *Early Christian Writings: The Apostolic Fathers*, trans. Maxwell Staniforth, rev. trans. Andrew Louth (New York: Penguin Classics, 1968), 123–32.

4. Characterizing the message of the Sermon on the Mount as defining the "Christian counter-culture" originated with John R. W. Stott. His classic work on Jesus' sermon is titled *Christian Counter-Culture: The Message of the Sermon on the Mount* (Downers Grove, IL: InterVarsity, 1978).

5. David J. Bosch, *Transforming Mission: Paradigm Shifts in Theology of Mission* (Maryknoll, NY: Orbis, 2011), 28. Emphasis added. "What amazes one again and again is the *inclusiveness* of Jesus' mission. It embraces both the poor and the rich, both the oppressed and the oppressor, both the sinners and the devout. His mission is one of dissolving alienation and breaking down walls of hostility, of crossing boundaries between individuals and groups. . . .The inclusiveness of Jesus' mission is highlighted particularly in the *Logia* or Sayings-Source. . . . There can be no doubt that a primary concern of the *Logia* is the preaching of love even to enemies in order that, if at all possible, such enemies may be won over. . . . The injunction to love one's enemies has rightly been described as the most characteristic saying of Jesus (references in Senior and Stuhlmueller 1983:159). Even Lapide (1986:91), an Orthodox Jew, says this was 'an innovation introduced by Jesus,'" 28–29.

6. This phrase is lifted from Goppelt's *Commentary on 1 Peter* (235): "The eschatological salvation is encountered as blessing because it is mediated through the active consolation of God. . . . Because they have been called to receive the consolation of salvation, the addressees are also able to respond to their opponents only with blessing. . . . Whoever meets an opponent as one who is destined to be '*a fellow heir of the grace of life*' (3:7) is acting as one who blesses." Emphasis added.

7. My Sudanese refugee friend's name has been changed to protect his privacy.

8. There are some contexts where being "blessed" by God *does* indicate being "approved" by him. In the Beatitudes, those who are "blessed" are those who have been welcomed into the Kingdom of God. So it is true that in that context, those who are "blessed" by God are those who are "saved" by God. In the next chapter, we'll explore how God's blessing ultimately dovetails with salvation. But this specific kind of blessing that has soteriological implications doesn't cancel out God's common blessing of all that sustains life in the world, as Jesus demonstrates in Luke 6:35-36.

9. Dietrich Bonhoeffer, *The Cost of Discipleship* (New York: Simon & Schuster, 1959, 1995), 150.

10. Story and quote are recounted in James H. Cone, *The Cross and the Lynching Tree* (Maryknoll, NY: Orbis, 2011, 2017), 78–79. Emphasis added.

11. Martin Luther King Jr., "Address at the Fiftieth Annual NAACP Convention," in *The Papers of Martin Luther King, Jr.*, ed. Clayborne Carson, vol. 5, Threshold of a New Decade, January 1959–December 1960 (Berkeley, CA: University of California Press, 2005), 247.

12. Martin Luther King Jr., *I Have a Dream: Writings and Speeches that Changed the World*, ed. James M. Washington (San Francisco: HarperOne, 2003), 22–23.

13. Asher Finkel, "Prayer in Jewish Life of the First Century as Background to Early Christianity," in *Into God's Presence: Prayer in the New Testament*, ed. Richard N. Longenecker (Grand Rapids, MI: Eerdmans, 2001), 48.

14. John O'Donohue, *To Bless the Space Between Us: A Book of Blessings* (New York: Doubleday, 2008), 206.

CHAPTER 9: BLESSING THAT CANCELS CURSE

1. Willa Cather, *Death Comes for the Archbishop* (New York: Random House, 1990), 4.

2. When Andres Serrano discussed the meaning of the work in an interview, he said his intention was to draw attention to the meaning of the cross, not to defame it: "The only message is that I'm a Christian artist making a religious work of art based on my relationship with Christ and The Church. The crucifix is a symbol that has lost its true meaning; the horror

of what occurred. It represents the crucifixion of a man who was tortured, humiliated and left to die on a cross for several hours. In that time, Christ not only bled to death, he probably saw all his bodily functions and fluids come out of him. So if 'Piss Christ' upsets people, maybe this is so because it is bringing the symbol closer to its original meaning." Udoka Okafor, "Exclusive Interview with Andres Serrano, Photographer of 'Piss Christ,'" *Huffington Post*, June 4, 2014, https://www.huffingtonpost.com/udoka -okafor/exclusive-interview-with-_18_b_5442141.html.

3. Some English translations obscure this detail by translating the Greek word *xulon* as "cross," but the ESV, KJV, and HCSB (among others) all retain the original word *tree*.

4. John R. W. Stott, *The Cross of Christ* (Downers Grove, IL: InterVarsity, 2006), 39. Emphasis added.

5. See N. T. Wright, *The Climax of the Covenant: Christ and the Law in Pauline Theology* (Minneapolis: Fortress, 1993), 144–47, for an enlightening discussion of the law in Deuteronomy and its application to the community as a whole with regards to Paul's reference to it in Galatians 3.

6. Matthew 27:46 references Psalm 22, a psalm that begins in lament but concludes in triumph. Jesus' cry contains a foreshadowing of his ultimate victory over death.

7. Simone Weil, *Waiting for God*, trans. Emma Craufurd (New York: Harper Collins, 2001), 72.

8. Martin Luther, *Commentary on the Epistle to the Galatians*, accessed November 20, 2018, http://www.gutenberg.org/files/1549/1549-h/1549 -h.htm#link2HCH0003. Emphasis added.

9. Miroslav Volf, *Free of Charge: Giving and Forgiving in a Culture Stripped of Grace* (Grand Rapids, MI: Zondervan, 2005), 145.

10. Peter's phrase is a quotation of Isaiah 53:5 in the Septuagint, with only slight changes that don't alter the meaning.

11. Otfried Hofius, "The Fourth Servant Song in the New Testament Letters," in *The Suffering Servant: Isaiah 53 in Jewish and Christian Sources*, ed. Bernd Janowski and Peter Stuhlmacher, trans. Daniel P. Bailey (Grand Rapids, MI: Eerdmans, 2004), 186.

12. To read more about Saint Matthew's Cross, see https://canmore.org.uk /event/921735.

13. Claus Westermann suggests that the expression "blessing of Christ" in Romans 15:29 indicates both God's saving *and* sustaining work. It suggests that the proclamation of the gospel brings about not only the salvation but also the growth and strengthening of the community (Claus Westermann, *Blessing in the Bible and the Life of the Church* (Philadelphia: Fortress, 1978), 99.

CHAPTER 10: TRANSFORMATION

1. Annie Dillard, *Three by Annie Dillard: Pilgrim at Tinker Creek, An American Childhood, and The Writing Life* (New York: Harper Perennial Classics, 2001), 104, 70.
2. Gordon J. Wenham, *Genesis 1-15*, Word Biblical Commentary (Waco, TX: Word, 1987), 65. Wenham confirms that "the picture of a great river flowing out of Eden is akin to Ps 46:5 . . . and Ezekiel's description of the eschatological Jerusalem from which a great river will flow to sweeten the Dead Sea (Ezek 47:1-12)," and that its meaning symbolizes God's presence.
3. Bruce K. Waltke with Cathi J. Fredricks, *Genesis: A Commentary* (Grand Rapids, MI: Zondervan, 2001), 447.
4. Isaiah 2:4, 11:6-7, 55:1, 65:25, Malachi 4:2, Jeremiah 31:12, Revelation 22:17 (author's paraphrase), Ezekiel 47:1-12.

READING AND REFLECTION GUIDE

1. G. B. Caird, *The Language and Imagery of the Bible* (Philadelphia: Westminster Press, 1980), 111.

THE NAVIGATORS® STORY

THANK YOU for picking up this NavPress book! I hope it has been a blessing to you.

NavPress is a ministry of The Navigators. The Navigators began in the 1930s, when a young California lumberyard worker named Dawson Trotman was impacted by basic discipleship principles and felt called to teach those principles to others. He saw this mission as an echo of 2 Timothy 2:2: "And the things you have heard me say in the presence of many witnesses entrust to reliable people who will also be qualified to teach others" (NIV).

In 1933, Trotman and his friends began discipling members of the US Navy. By the end of World War II, thousands of men on ships and bases around the world were learning the principles of spiritual multiplication by the intentional, person-to-person teaching of God's Word.

After World War II, The Navigators expanded its relational ministry to include college campuses; local churches; the Glen Eyrie Conference Center and Eagle Lake Camps in Colorado Springs, Colorado; and neighborhood and citywide initiatives across the country and around the world.

Today, with more than 2,600 US staff members—and local ministries in more than 100 countries—The Navigators continues the transformational process of making disciples who make more disciples, advancing the Kingdom of God in a world that desperately needs the hope and salvation of Jesus Christ and the encouragement to grow deeper in relationship with Him.

NavPress was created in 1975 to advance the calling of The Navigators by bringing biblically rooted and culturally relevant products to people who want to know and love Christ more deeply. In January 2014, NavPress entered an alliance with Tyndale House Publishers to strengthen and better position our rich content for the future. Through *THE MESSAGE* Bible and other resources, NavPress seeks to bring positive spiritual movement to people's lives.

If you're interested in learning more or becoming involved with The Navigators, go to www.navigators.org. For more discipleship content from The Navigators and NavPress authors, visit www.thedisciplemaker.org. May God bless you in your walk with Him!

Sincerely,

DON PAPE
VP/PUBLISHER, NAVPRESS

www.navpress.com

CP1308